The Wide Awake Club - Solutions for Knackered Parents

Fi Star-Stone

Copyright © 2020 Fi Star-Stone

Illustrated by Orla Hope Fielder

ISBN: 9798642271926

Other books by Fi Star-Stone:

The Baby Bedtime book - Say goodnight to Sleepless nights

The Wide Awake Kids Club

My 'Thinky-Thoughts' Journal

CONTENTS

DEDICATION

To my lovely little family, Richie, Betsy and Oscar and my folks, aka Trish and Mike, who always support my dreams and make me cups of tea, while I work into the small hours tapping away to get my books finished.

To my best mate Ceri who listens to my worries and self-doubt and reassures me always with kindness and gin.

Special thanks to a lovely family in London (The Hoffmanns) who will always have a special place in my heart.

To my BMC crew who are always supportive and celebrate every success and catch every fall. Thanks girls - See you on the dance-floor soon!

Fi xx

INTRODUCTION

Hello lovely face!

Firstly, thanks for purchasing this little baby sleep guide of mine. I really hope the gentle techniques, tips and information, help your family create healthy sleep habits that last, because, let's face it - sleep is one of the most important needs in life. Without sleep, we begin to suffer both physically and mentally, (car keys in the fridge anyone?)

If your little love is a fully fledged member of *The Wide Awake Baby Club* - don't worry, you're not alone! From wide-awakers that refuse to go to bed, to midnight baby bed-invaders, I've been overwhelmed with requests for solutions to solving bedtime issues over the years, from thousands of parents all over the world.

This inspired me to write my very first book 'The Baby Bedtime Book - Say Goodnight to Sleepless nights' over five years ago. The book became a bestseller in its category and to this day *still* helps so many parents with sleep.

I love my first child sleep book, but it is important to me that I always keep up to date with the latest research including my own, and to update new tips and ideas that have worked for my clients.

Parenting and childcare has changed over the years, and even in the 25 years I've been working with families I've seen a huge shift in sleep, weaning and baby care advice. The basics stay the same - but the world grows and changes and I like to keep up with those changes and adapt my advice to suit the busy lives parents live today.

I also feel that baby and toddler sleep is very different - so I wanted to split the two into two brand new books to make it easier to read, easier to understand and more relevant to each age group.

This little book covers baby sleep up to 12 months, and my next book covers the toddler years 12 months - 3 years.

You've likely bought this baby sleep guide because you're totally knackered and want a quick-fix magic solution to your baby's sleep issues. I'll be brutally honest - although I've been told often that I'm magical in my methods - there really is no quick fix when it comes to sleep. It takes time, patience and a whole lot of consistency. I give the tips - but it is you, the parent, that does the hard work and therefor deserves the praise and reward.

Without wanting to sound like a total 'expert bore-off,' being consistent and is crucial to make any of the techniques in this book work. Everyone involved in your baby's life needs to be on the same page. All of you need to follow the same plan, same rules and to all be consistent, otherwise it just won't work.

You don't need to read this book cover to cover, you can of course skip to the good bits, or the chapters you feel are relevant to your baby, but I honestly think if you read it all the way through, (I have kept it as short and snappy as possible - apart from this bit because if I can't go on about myself in my own book - when can I?) Then the tips and the thoughts and reasoning behind them, will make so much more sense if you do.

In the back of this book, I've included some helpful websites and numbers and also some pages for you to jot down your own routine and feeds and any notes you might like to make while reading this book.

Without another word of ramble, let's begin the journey to better sleep for you all.

CHAPTER ONE: THE NEW BABY CLUB: HOW TO COPE AND KEEP YOUR COOL IN THE FIRST FEW WEEKS.

A favourite track of mine by the wonderful *Faithless,* seems to be the anthem of parents worldwide. 'I can't get no sleep!' (do-der, do-do-der, do-do-der, do-do-der- deh!)

Tiredness is horrible, I do understand as a mum myself.

Becoming a parent for the first time in 2009 was an emotional explosion. All my ideas of parenthood floated out of the window! Working with families for all the year I had - I stupidly thought it would be breeze.

Don't get me wrong, the first few days of being a mum were fantastic. My labour started as a chilled home birth, in a birthing pool in my front room in South East London. After 12 hours, I was transferred to hospital due to complications, but on arrival - our little girl Betsy, was born naturally in Lewisham Hospital.

In the days that followed my body ached, my bits hurt, my boobs were sore, and I felt such a mess, but my beautiful little first-born slept like a dream. She breastfed perfectly and life was sweet. This parenting business was so easy! Or so I thought.

After two weeks, my little newborn showed me what crying in the early hours with silent reflux was all about. she taught me the feeling of exhaustion and Like most parents I had to manage on little sleep. I was a full on Mombie. My daughter taught me that parenting wasn't anything like teaching pre-schoolers or nannying tiny babies. Caring for other people's children was a whole different ball game. Firstly - you got to hand them back at the end of the day and go do your whole child-free thing. second - you arrived each day bright eyed full of energy after an uninterrupted nights' sleep.

Becoming a parent can take some getting used to. You are handed this little bundle and sent on your way to manage. It is hugely overwhelming - it is often terrifying, and there is SO much information out there it can be mind blowing.

I want to say to you - that the few weeks are just about finding your feet. Your baby's first weeks are about adapting to your new role as a parent and just getting through, and to enjoying that whole new baby bubble' as you adapt to the the new life you are starting. Those days hit you in a way you can't really prepare for so please just go with the flow and forget about routine.

Those glorious first days with your newborn should be a time for enjoying every precious minute with your new bundle of joy, but often those days go by in a whirlwind of feeding, nappy changing and visits from family, so to start this little sleep book, to help you manage those first precious week, I've started the book with my top ten 'I've just had a baby' life hacks to survive those early days!

Ten 'I've just had a baby' life hacks:

1. **Food frenzy!** BEFORE little one arrives – stock up the freezer with easy meals to heat up or cake loaves for visitors! (The cake one: We all know cake is good for the soul right? It also makes you look pretty awesome – visitors won't know they've been made weeks before!) Ideally this is great if you're reading this while awaiting baby's arrival, but if not - when you do next cook a meal - bulk up and freeze the leftovers. you'll be thankful of those freezer meals when times get tough or you're feeling really knackered. Take-aways are great in moderation, but they're expensive and not ideal daily.

2. **Buy in bulk!** Stock up on baby essentials like the apocalypse (or pandemic) is about to happen. Seriously – make sure you have enough nappies, wipes and baby bits and bobs *before* baby arrives. The last thing you'll feel like doing after just having a baby is nipping to the shops for nappy cream! If you've not done this and little one is already here - sort yourself a regular online delivery slot or amazon grocery slot to make sure you'll not run out of those essentials. If due to finances, your shopping is more of a weekly thing - look out online for deals. Supermarkets often have ,baby events' where you bulk buy nappies or wipes or cotton pads and save a small fortune.

3. **Prepare your replies!** Keeping in touch is awesome - but when you've just ad a baby it can be exhausting keeping up with well-wishers! so, prepare a text reply on your smart phone for those lovely well wishers that keep calling because they can't wait to see the new baby!
Something like 'Thanks so much for calling - busy with our new little one at the moment but will call you back as soon as hands are free!' Most smartphones have an option to create a text reply to save when people call.

It's a great way of responding to calls when you have your hands full and are busy with little one, have other visitors or just need a little space. It means callers won't keep bombarding you with calls and answer-phone messages!

4. **It's about how you *feel* not how you look!** Forget about the left-over baby bump if you have just given birth! Ignore the instagram glam and baby magazines with body perfect 'mum models' on the front - it's not real. Please don't focus on the whole 'getting your pre-baby body back culture that stream social media. Focus on the here and now and enjoy the time.

That beautiful belly bump of yours will hang around for a while - so please embrace it. You grew a whole baby! (Or some of you may have grown more than one in one go or had one, or two before!) Give yourself a break!

I'd also love you to take a look at some really body positive accounts on social media, especially accounts by mums who have had babies and embrace their figures like a friend of mine, Molly Forbes. You may have seen Molly presenting TV's *Naked Beach*. (The Channel 4 reality shows people with body insecurities jet to a sunny island to spend time with body-confident naked people, covered only with paint.) Your physical appearance *doesn't* matter - but how you feel *does!* I don't know about you, but for me, getting dressed and doing my teeth and putting something other than PJ's or joggers - makes me feel good.

PJ days are awesome, of course they are, but honestly? Having a shower, brushing teeth and getting dressed, makes me feel more awake and ready for the day. It's good for my mental health. Listen up, even if you won't be leaving the house, getting dressed changes your mindset and makes you feel ready for the day.

New Dads - This is for you too! You're going to be feeling knackered too and perhaps not feel like making an effort. I don't want to sound like a mum here - but have a shave mate (unless you have a beard of course - I don't want to start a relationship war here 'that sleep consultant told me to have my beard off') Brush your teeth, put some comfy clean clothes on and ditch the jammies during the day. It honestly, really really helps with that knackered feeling.

Whatever your family unit, two mums, two dads, mum and dad or single parent, make yourself feel a little brighter by getting up and at em' and ready for the day.

There is always a way to do this! Take it in turns with your partner to have that 'getting ready' time, or invest in a baby chair and take baby into the bathroom with you. A shower takes 5 minutes tops in a rush and 10 minutes if baby is sleeping and it'll make your day feel so much nicer.

5. **Prepare for the escape!** The first few days you'll likely want to hang around the house adjusting to parenthood, but getting out and about after a few days is so good for you! Even just a walk to the park. So – prepare that nappy bag! Honestly don't go out with the essentials. I've been there - and it's not pretty! (Poo explosion nappy during a pub lunch was not fun.)

Have a bag always ready with things you may need for your baby (And don't forget things for you! Spare clothes in case of baby mom on your top, money, phone, keys, etc.)

If you use an item, make sure you replace it as soon as you can, that way your bag is always ready – you can pop out anytime without a mad rush to scram everything into a bag and end up forgetting things! you don't need a fancy-pants changing bag either. Invest in a big bag or rucksack and use that - you honestly don't need expensive nappy bags. Save your cash!

6. **Set up a changing box downstairs.** That gorgeous nursery you spent hours making beautiful and instagram-likes worthy? The changing station all decorated and organised beautifully? It'll likely only get used mornings and at bedtime if you live in a house rather than a flat. So – invest in a little basket of changing goodies for downstairs. It makes life easier.

It'll save your legs when you are shattered (or sore,) stairs are hard work with a baby when you're feeling shattered. It's also fab if someone offers to change a nappy - they won't see the explosion of messy 'I've just had a baby' chaos upstairs! It keeps the visitors where you want them! Clever hey?

7. **Perfect your knowing nod.** Seriously - you'll likely get more advice in the first week of becoming a parent than all the years that follow. So, to avoid family feuds, broken friendships or in extreme cases – getting arrested – perfect your *'thanks for the advice now P*ss off'* face and use it anytime someone offers unsolicited advice.

Say nothing.

Nod knowingly.

Smile. (Rant freely when they've gone!)

8. **Eat Cake.** It makes you happy. Seriously – Please don't start a 'drop the baby weight' diet in those first few weeks. Eat well, eat healthily too when and where you can, but don't deny yourself those treats.

Tiredness sucks. Cake is nice and makes you smile (or biscuits – or whatever treat you fancy.) Please remember to be kind to yourself.

9. **Take time out.** I see you laugh at this one, and I do know as a parent myself - it's not easy, but - it's essential. Even a bath and a book for half an hour each week if you can. Ask your partner, your family – even your friends to help you have that 'me time' and you'll feel a million times better and able to handle whatever this parenting rollercoaster throws at you.

Maybe for a walk on your own, lie on the bed listening to music or watching a favourite TV show. Read a bit of a book at a time for a bit of escapism. Just half an hour of 'time off' from parenthood will do you so much good. Oh – and don't feel guilty about it either! Parenting is totally lovely but take time for you and you'll parent even better! Ask for help so you can have your half an hour. (Anything over half an hour and you're winning!)

10. **Buy twenty-million Burp cloths:** You can honestly never have too many burp/sicky cloths! They are great for mopping up spills, protecting your clothes while feeding, protecting your favourite rug from baby sick (placed underneath baby) used as a cover while breastfeeding in public if you're prefer to cover-up, used for peekaboo games, for collecting baby toys up and wrapping into a sack. They can even be used in an emergency *'what do you mean we've run out of nappies'* drama!

These simple tips aren't anything life-changing (although I have had a few parents saying they really were at one point,) but they can make life a little easier while you're finding your feet as a new parent.

Now let's get on to the main focus of this book and the reason why you bought it! My simple solutions for knackered parents!

Newborn babies invariably wake up repeatedly in the night for the first few months, and disturbed nights can be very hard to cope with. As the weeks go by there are lots of reasons your little one will wake and this can result in feeling totally zombified the next day.

Despite being a Child Sleep Consultant I've had many sleepless nights caused by illness, teething or nightmares. I'm such a grump without good sleep and I just can't function properly. To help you with those early weeks and sleepless nights throughout your parenting journey, and before we go onto sleep tips, I wanted to share some things that have helped new parents who came to me for help and helped me survive those early parenting days with little sleep.

Shower power!

Guess what? I am not a morning person. Even when I've had good sleep I find it hard to jump out of bed and dance around, full of the joys of Spring, unlike my lovely family who seem to always be bright eyed and bushy tailed whatever sleep they've had! The main thing (apart from coffee) that sorts me out is a hot shower! If I'm particularly knackered - a cool shower is the business!

When you are totally shattered, especially in those early days - it is so very tempting to hang out in your PJs all day and not get changed, do your teeth or brush your hair, and while I totally love a PJ day, I have to say a shower and fresh clothes will make you feel so much better about facing the day ahead. I know I've already covered this in my 'Parenting hacks' small chapter - but it's important to mention it again.

I find a nice smelling shower gel works magic! There are three scents that can really wake you up:

Jasmine, which increases beta waves (the brain waves associated with alertness), and citrus and peppermint scents, which stimulate the same nerve that's activated when you're revived with smelling salts!

Coffee: I'm going against the advice of every healthy eating guide ever published here, but enjoying a good cup of coffee helps keep tiredness at bay. I'm not suggesting caffeine overdrive here, just a little happy perk-me-up to keep you going through the day.

If you are breastfeeding, and want to avoid caffeine, even just smelling coffee can give you a boost. In experiments with exhausted laboratory rats, *han-Seok Seo* found that coffee aroma helps reduce the stress of sleep deprivation. Clever eh? So sniff those coffee beans my lovelies for that wide-awake feeling and put the knackered parent brain on pause.

Eat Well!

Without wanting to echo my lovely Nanna aged 92 who still follows her own advice - 'always start the day with a good breakfast!' The last thing you feel like doing when you are exhausted is eating properly - I do understand, but a healthy breakfast; believe me, will set you up for the day after an awful night.

I'm guilty of reaching for the pastry or even biscuit tin when I'm shattered - and in moderation this is fine, but when sleepless nights keep you up over and over, especially as a new parent - you need to fuel that tired body of yours.

Did you know eating an hour after waking (on what little sleep you have had) will make you feel more alert and ready for the day ahead? True story. So instead of the coco pops or blueberry muffin - go for a breakfast that contains slow energy releasing carbohydrates like porridge with raisins for an extra sugar boost! It will soon have you feeling more human.

Energy boosting foods: For meals throughout the day (and it's important to repeat an earlier sentiment about remembering to eat suing the day and have regular meals) go for foods that will help you with that Mombie or Zomdad feeling.

These foods in particular offer some energy boosting magic:

Sweet potato: Sweet potato is high in carbohydrates and loaded with vitamin A and vitamin C. Make into little homemade dips to dip in hummus or serve as a jacket potato with beans!

Honey: Did you know that a spoonful of honey is nature's equivalent of an energy drink? Smart eh? Not only is it a slow time release
energy food, it's also great for a sweet kick instead of sugar. Add to your

morning porridge, yogurt or add a few drops to your afternoon cuppa for a little boost.

Bananas: Well know as a healthy treat, bananas are an easy snack to carry around with you in your bag! Great for a mid-morning break or to slice and pop on your breakfast!

Almonds: These magical energy snacks are packed with protein, manganese, copper and riboflavin! Copper and manganese play
an essential role in keeping energy flowing throughout the body and Riboflavin aids oxygen-based energy production.

My Bad night booster!

This fatigue fighting bad night booster is both nutritious and delicious and filled with energy boosting ingredients. great for fighting the Zombie parent days! so many of the parents I've shared it with have said it really is a mood and energy booster!

The *'Bad night booster'* will give you that little kick you need after an awful night's sleep. It's also quite a fab drink when you have a cold too - so great for when you're feeling under the weather!

I've popped the recipe on the next below. Advance warning - You'll need a blender or smoothie maker to make this!

Banana Bad-night-Booster

Ingredients: (makes two smoothies)

2 x Bananas
2 x tsp honey
2 x tsp cinnamon powder
2 x pint semi-skimmed milk, Soya, Oat or Almond milk.

Method:

Chop the banana and add all the ingredients into a blender. Add ice too for a real wake-up kick! blend until smooth.

Add more milk/Soya if too thick for your liking.

Did you know that a spoonful of honey is nature's equivalent of an energy drink? Not only is it a slow time release energy food, it's also great for a sweet kick instead of sugar.

Banana is a nice, slow releasing energy food and the cinnamon gives it the taste kick that not only improves the body's ability to utilise blood sugar, but the smell boosts brain activity too! This really is a clever little smoothie to give a boost after a bad night with your *Wide Awake Baby Club* member!

Other Mombie/Zomdad tips include;

Have a power nap!

Sounds amazing right? I see you rolling your eyes to the age-old advice of 'sleeping when the baby sleeps' but honestly - it is so important to listen to your body! Forget that you have a million and one things to do - are they as important as your health? Nope.
Please listen to me. Take the power nap! A quick 30 minute cat-nap will make such a difference to your mind and your body.

Get some fresh air: Fresh air is just the best remedy for super-shattered parents I promise! Going out for a walk with your newborn is probably the last thing you feel like doing when exhausted, but it's seriously good for you and your baby! We have two dogs, so for me a daily walk is already part of my routine.

On days that follow tough nights where I've been up with poorly kids or working helping parents during the night, or ya' know - Netflix binges that lasted til' 3am - those walks save me! In fact - I'm not long back from our' one walk a day' lockdown walk with the little ones and dogs - and it's boosted me to keep writing today.

Socialise! I'm not talking a quick half down the local, although that's nice on a weekend too, I mean get together with fellow parents for a cuppa. If you've made friends at your local baby group or during your pregnancy get together with them during the rubbish no-sleep days.

It's great to chat about the bad night-times. It's incredibly therapeutic and you'll most likely find they are going through the same thing too. If getting out and about is hard - video call friends. Talk on social media is great - but face-to-face interactions are important for good mental health.

Get an early night: I'm not suggesting a spot of *romancing* here - (although enjoying sexual intimacy improves your mood by releasing feel good endorphins.) It can also help you sleep, lower your blood pressure, boost your immunity, alleviate pain and reduce stress too. So if you're up for a bit of Netflix and chill - go for it.

I suspect however, like many knackered parents - it's the furthest thing from your mind right now, in which case early nights are great for getting a few more hours shut-eye.

Early nights are also great for early sleep. Even a couple of nights a week getting into bed with a book and switching off the screen time will give you a real boost and help you cope with the long nights that often come with the early weeks of parenting. Please take 'catching up on sleep' out of your head.

Honestly just forget all of the bad nights and focus on the new nights to come. You'll drive yourself crazy with the thought of playing sleep catch-up. There is no real way to recoup lost sleep, only things you can do to look after yourself if you're feeling sleep deprived, or to improve your future sleep and hopefully this book will help with that!

So now I've prepped you to feel less knackered - let's look at how much sleep your baby needs according to their age.

CHAPTER THREE: WHY IS SLEEP IMPORTANT AND HOW MUCH DOES MY BABY NEED?

As parents, we all have, at some stage, known how it feels to be sleep deprived and how unwell it makes us feel. We also know we need decent sleep to live a happy, healthy life. But what does sleep actually do?

According to the *National Institute of Neurological Disorders and Stroke* (NINDS,) Sleep affects almost every type of tissue and system in the body - from the brain, heart, and lungs to metabolism, immune function, mood, and disease resistance.

Research shows that a chronic lack of sleep, or getting poor quality sleep, increases the risk of disorders including high blood pressure, cardiovascular disease, diabetes, depression, and obesity, so setting up good sleep habits now will not only benefit your little one now, but in the future too.

Babies, (and children teens) need significantly more sleep than adults to support their rapid mental and physical development. A recent *study suggests sleep and episodic length growth in 4-17 month-old infants to be a temporally coupled process with prolonged sleep preceding length growth by 0-4 days. The authors found an increase of up to 4.5 hours and/or three more naps per day to be predictive of length growth suggesting an underlying biological system.

During the early weeks your baby is likely to doze off for short periods during a feed, don't worry - this is normal. Some babies sleep much more than others, some sleep for long periods, others in short bursts. Every baby is different, but as your baby grows older (from 3 months) they have the ability to sleep for 8 hours or longer at night.

Be prepared to change routines as your baby grows and enters different stages. And remember, growth spurts, teething and illnesses can all affect how your baby sleeps.

Don't worry if yours isn't sleeping for those amount of hours yet - the gentle tips and guidance in this little book will help you on your way to better nights.

As a guide here is the amount of sleep your baby needs during the first two years.

Newborn sleep

Most newborn babies are asleep more than they are awake. Their total daily sleep varies, but can be from 8 hours up to 16 or 18 hours.

During this age - Babies will wake during the night because they need to be fed, because they are uncomfortable, and because they don't know the difference between night and day yet.

Age	Daytime	Nightime	Average Total Sleep
1 - 3 months	8 (varied amount of naps)	9	17

3 to 6 months old sleep

As your baby grows, they'll need fewer night feeds and will be able to sleep for longer. They'll be learning the difference between night and day and will sleep for 8 hours or longer at night when in a routine.

Usually by 4 months old, they are spending around double the amount of hours at night as they sleep in the day, but this can be disturbed by discomfort, teething,

Age	Daytime	Nightime	Average Total Sleep
3 - 6 months	6 (varied amount naps, now more structured)	10	16

6 to 12 months old sleep

For babies aged 6 months to a year have the ability to sleep for up to 12 hours at night. They are still having 2-3 naps during the day until round 9 months when they drop to 2 naps.

Most babies will have long dropped the night feeds now, but teething, discomfort, hunger or separation anxiety (more on that later,) may wake some babies during the night or make it hard for them to settle at bedtime.

Age	Daytime	Nightime	Average Total Sleep
6-9 months	3 (2-3 routine naps)	12	15
9-12 months	3 (2 routine naps)	12	15

A look at things to come: 12 - 18 months old sleep

Babies will sleep for around 12 to 15 hours in total after their first birthday. By this age they drop down to one nap during the day. Again, teething, discomfort, illness, hunger or separation anxiety, (more on that later) may wake some babies during the night or make it hard for them to settle at bedtime.

Age	Daytime	Nightime	Average Total Sleep
12-18 months	2 (1 routine naps)	12	14

Remember that every baby is different and this hours of sleep needed is just a guide. Try not to worry if your baby sleeps differently to others - and please don't go by the advice of family and friends on how much (or little) *their* babies slept.

Unless your baby *rarely wakes up* - even to eat, there is most likely no reason to worry that your baby is sleeping too much. Remember - in those early weeks your bay will sleep a lot!

All babies change their sleep patterns at some point, and just when you think you have it sorted and you've all had a good night's sleep, the next night you might be up every hour with a fully fledged member of the *Wide Awake Baby Club!*

In my next book 'The Wide Awake toddlers Club' we'll look into the difference between baby and toddler sleep, and the new problems that often arise during the toddler years.

CHAPTER FOUR: THE COOL CRIB BRIGADE - CREATING A SAFE AND COMFORTABLE SLEEP SPACE FOR BABY.

We've all had that bad night sleep before becoming parents. You know, the sleepover at a friends house where you just can't get comfy?

Maybe you've been the second child who got the hand-me-down lumpy mattress from their older sibling, or the kid that had the coldest room in the house? Maybe you've been a guest at a night over for a family event, lodged between the ironing board and bookcase?

So - you see, it's a no-brainer that to be able to sleep well, you need to be comfortable. (Unless you're my husband who could probably sleep standing up in a hurricane.)

Rather than rattle on about comfort, here's a nice little checklist to getting a better sleep space for your baby and thus - better sleep for you all! Tadaa!

Buy a good quality and safe cot/crib and mattress

When shopping for your baby's bed - cheap usually means rubbish (take it from this bargain queen who regrets a recent purchase online!)
You should use a firm and flat mattress that is protected by a waterproof cover. This will help keep the mattress clean and dry, as the cover can be wiped down.

Make sure your baby's mattress is in good condition and that it fits the Moses basket or cot properly. For safety reasons you shouldn't use a second hand mattress either.

A good quality mattress should serve your baby throughout their baby years until they move from their cot to their toddler bed. Splash the cash on a safe, decent cot and mattress if you can. It really is worth it. If money is tight - safety is the most important thing here - so check safety standards before paying out for your baby's bed or crib.

To Co-sleep or not?

Babies ideally should be slept in a clear sleep space, which is easy to create in a cot or Moses basket. However, I know that many families also choose to bed share, and so I wanted to include *The Lullaby Trust's* guidance when it comes to co-sleeping.

Their recommendations for making your bed a safer place for baby whether you doze off accidentally, or choose to bed share is below:

• Keep pillows, sheets, blankets away from your baby or any other items that could obstruct your baby's breathing or cause them to overheat. A high proportion of infants who die as a result of SIDS are found with their head covered by loose bedding.

• Ensure baby is sleeping baby on their back
• Avoid letting pets or other children in the bed
• Make sure baby won't fall out of bed or get trapped between the mattress and the wall

When not to co-sleep

It is important for you to know that there are some circumstances in which co-sleeping with your baby can be very dangerous:

• Either you or your partner smokes (even if you do not smoke in the bedroom)
• Either you or your partner has drunk alcohol or taken drugs (including medications that may make you drowsy)
• You are extremely tired
• Your baby was born premature (37 weeks or less)
• Your baby was born at a low weight (2.5kg or 5½ lbs or less)
• Never sleep on a sofa or armchair with your baby, this can increase the risk of SIDS by 50 times

You should never sleep together with your baby if any of the above points apply to you or your partner.

Another way of achieving that close, co-sleeping bond in a much safer way is to invest in a cot that attaches to your bed known as a 'bedside crib.'

Bedside cribs

A bedside crib is a bassinet-style cot that affixes to your bed, with one side that can be removed or dropped down and out of the way so that you can easily lift your baby out towards you for middle-of-the-night feeding, or if you need to soothe them back to sleep.

Official 'safe sleeping' guidance from the NHS advises that your newborn sleeps in the same room as you for the first six months, but not in your bed, due to the risk of suffocation and overheating. A bedside crib offers you the benefits of co-sleeping, but with the added safety of them having their own space. Bedside cots are usually suitable from birth up until your baby is around six months old, or when they can start to pull themselves up to sitting.

If you do decide to invest in a bedside crib - it's important to measure your bed before purchasing. This will ensure there's no gap between your baby's mattress and your own, and that the crib can be securely attached to your bed. Check that the crib's mattress height adjusts to the same level as your own mattress, and triple-check compatibility as some cribs are designed to clip onto bedstead frames and therefore won't work with a divan style bed.

Invest in good bedding

Fancy bedding isn't needed, nor are cot bumpers or pillows, (pillow use alone has been shown to increase the chance of SIDS occurring by up to 2.5 times) but *comfortable and safe* bedding is.

If using a 'baby sleeping bag' always check the tog and change for the time of year to avoid baby overheating or getting too cold.

Firmly tucked in sheets and blankets (not above shoulder height) or a baby sleep bag are safe for a baby to sleep in. Be sure to remove any soft toys from the cot before your baby goes to sleep. the emptier the cot - the safer the sleeping space.

Blankets are ok for chillier nights BUT always make sure they are firmly tucked in.

Room temperature

The temperature of the room where your baby is sleeping definitely affects your their sleep so it's worth investing in a room thermometer for younger children.

It is important to make sure that your baby's room is a comfortable temperature – not too hot or too cold. The chance of SIDS is higher in babies who get too hot, so try to keep the room temperature between 16 -20°C

with young babies - it's important to check they're not too hot. Feel your baby's tummy or the back of their neck rather than their hands which naturally always feel cooler.

If your baby's skin is hot or they are sweaty, remove one or more layers of bedclothes or bedding.

Room lighting

Although darkness is best for sleep (because when it's dark, we release melatonin, which relaxes the body.) you do need a little light to be able to check baby and to do night feeds.

Rather than having a pitch-black room, invest in a low light nightlight.

In Summer, when it's bright at your baby's bedtime - it's no surprise they may struggle to fall asleep. Black-out blinds are ideal for the spring clock changes, and you can even get stick on temporary ones if your budget is limited. Black out blinds often stop the early-riser waking up for early breakfast feeds!

The biggest no-no at bedtime when it comes to lighting, even for babies, are mobile phones and computer screens; These LED displays glow with blue light, which suppresses melatonin even more. It's one of the biggest causes of sleep issues that I help knackered parents of older children with. While i'm not suggesting your six month old has their own mobile already - it's best to avoid getting into the habit of being on your phone when doing bedtimes, or letting your little have any screens such as tablets playing lullabies.

Bedroom Sounds

I have good hearing and hear the slightest noise in the night and often wake my sleeping husband to tell him! He is always really thankful for this disturbance in his sleep.

Our children however, luckily haven't inherited their Mum's ability to be woken by a mouse walking on the path outside, and sleep soundly, like their dad, through storms, neighbours parties, and once an intruder in the garden that set the dogs off going bonkers. I think this is due to the fact we never tiptoed around them as babies so they have always have slept through noise. Even parties! (Not wild ones - those days are far behind me!

When it comes to night time - peace and quiet is great - but don't feel you need to have everything switched off and silent - especially if you are staying up to catch up on your Netflix season!

Having said this - some babies are highly sensitive to noise at night especially sudden or repetitive noises, and these can interrupt sleep and cause real issues night after night. Especially external sounds from the streets outside.

One of the best ways to combat outside noise is double glazing (I sound like a sales person now! I so should've got a sponsorship deal with a window company for this book!) Seriously though, good windows really do muffle sounds from outside - take it from someone who lived right on the South East London, South Circular. It was worth the investment for a good nights sleep night after night.

If replacing windows and doors (oh my life, I really do sound like a windows sales person,) isn't within your finances, then invest in some good quality blinds or thick curtains to muffle external sounds.

While some like to sleep in perfect-peace, others find certain sounds comforting. 'White noise' sounds are super beneficial for little babies, as are heartbeat sounds and gentle musical bedtime played on a baby sound soother near the cot (but to of reach and not too loud!) these kind of sounds can be really soothing and helpful for joining the land of nod.

Music, or sounds of forests or seasides, played softly through a small speaker can also help babies to feel relaxed and fall asleep.

Bedroom smells

A clean bedroom is a happy bedroom - this is what I tell my little ones and it's kinda sinking in. Well, almost.

To be fair to them, they are pretty cool, and they empty their bins once a week make their beds (definitely not instagram worth bed making skills - but made at least!) They put washing in the laundry bin when reminded and once a fortnight pull off the bedsheets for me to wash and change them (well trained hey?) Anyway - I digress. Sorry!

Let's face it - smelly sheets are not comfy sheets and babies bed sheets and sleeping bags get pretty gross quite quickly. To keep your baby's bedding clean and safe for them, you need to wash your baby's sheets at least twice a week. In some cases, it needs more washing if there is soiling present on them. Everyone loves clean-sheet day right?

Bedroom bins with stinky nappies are not nice environments to sleep in and it's these simple things that can create a good or bad nights sleep.

One thing I do love is the smell of lavender. While I'd avoid using a diffuser in your baby room (more on that in a minute) You can use it for baby massage after your baby's bath.

If you do choose to give lavender oil a try, please know that you cannot place it directly on your baby's skin because of its potency. Instead, the essential oil should be diluted with what is known as a carrier oil. To be safe - it's best to purchase 'baby friendly' lavender products that have already been tested safe to use on your little one.

Don't be tempted to mask smells using air fresheners or diffusers or plug-ins - especially for young babies.

Despite their popularity, there are concerns that these products increase indoor air pollution and pose a health risk, especially with long-term exposure. Air fresheners release volatile organic compounds (VOCs) into the air. A VOC is a type of chemical that turns into a vapour or gas easily at room temperature.

Health problems are thought to occur from the chemicals in the air fresheners and from their secondary pollutants. Secondary pollutants are formed when a product's chemicals combine with the ozone already in the air. Even when these products are used as directed, there are concerns about health problems with repeated exposure.

Make your baby's room smell clean and fresh by eliminating bad smells and you'll be creating the perfect smelling canvas for a great nights sleep.

However you choose to 'sleep zone' your baby's room - think about everything you've read in this book so far that creates a 'good sleeping environment' and make an informed choice on how to make it a perfect sleeping space for your little one.

CHAPTER FIVE: THE WIDE AWAKE BABY CLUB - WHY ROUTINE IS THE MAGIC KEY!

Routine is the magic key!

It's the phrase I'm kinda known for and one I say rather a lot. People @ me on social media with their happy bedtime stories of success; 'It works Fi - you're right! #RoutineIsTheMagicKey! Even my hairstylist says it to me when he's telling me how he's shared my books and website with his friends who are parents! (Thanks Steve!)

Of all the questions I get from parents, 'how can I get my baby into a routine?' seems to be the most frequent, and while routine really is, in my opinion, *the magic key* to ditching *Wide Awake Baby Club* membership - in those precious early days it's all about settling in and finding your feet a a new parent.

However, as the weeks pass by, it really is helpful to all of you as a family, to gradually implement a routine. You may feel ready to introduce a bedtime routine when your baby is around 3 months old. Getting them into a simple, comforting, happy bedtime routine can be helpful for the whole family and often prevents sleeping problems later on.

My own little ones and the families I've worked with, started a routine quite early on. Around 6 weeks old they were following my 'Four for Happiness' routine.

I know this is still hugely popular with parents and featured in my first book so I want to include it in this one too, but the new, updated version! my 'Four for Happiness' routine is ideal for formula fed *and* combined fed babies, and *some* breastfed babies too. My own breastfed little ones managed fall into the four hourly pattern really well too, but I know speaking to lots of other parents who breastfed, that a 3 hourly routine worked better for them and was more achievable.

Many parents choose to feed on demand in which case this routine won't work. Parenting really is about doing what works for you rather than following a schedule set by someone who doesn't know your child. So don't feel that what you choose to do is wrong, just because something is working for somebody else. Remember my phrase in the introduction of this book? *'every child is different and every family is different!' So please don't worry and don't compare your parenting to other families.*

'Fi's Four for Happiness – The baby routine'

When my second child Oscar, was born, less than a year after my daughter (I know! Crazy right?) I was still fining my feet a parent, but one thing I'd learned was my own advice given to many - really worked. (Who knew?!) Jokes aside, routine really is the magic key when it comes to ditching membership to the *Wide Awake Baby Club*. With two babies to look after - I had to follow routine otherwise I'd be completely and utterly exhausted! I followed my *'Four for happiness' routine that has been used by parents across the world!*

From New York to New Zealand, I've helped thousands of parents establish a routine by following a simple, gentle guide developed during my professional career.

Through my sleep research and my experiences working with families around the world, learned that all babies and parents are different, and that what works for one, just won't work with another, but one thing has always really really stuck out. *Routine* was the magical key to a good night's sleep.

Over the years I've been lucky to have a varied working life working with lots of different families and children in different roles. Working night shifts as a maternity nurse in my early career, I learned about sleep patterns both by observing the little ones in my care, and through reading sleep research from around the world. I talked with sleep consultants, other childcare professionals and spent my free time reading up on new sleep practices. They all had the thing in common - ***routine works.***

As a professional nanny and then, as a mum myself, I noticed that the nearer to four hourly feeds babies got, the better they were at sleeping through the night.

Whether you decided to breastfeed, combine feed or formula feed your baby, there are two methods in which your baby feeds. These methods are demand feeding and routine feeding.

Feeding on demand V Routine feeding

Many new parents ask me if they should be feeding on demand (following baby's signal that they're hungry)) or feeding on a schedule (feeding baby at timed intervals for a specific length of time) My answer is simple - you have to do what you feel is right.

Some babies thrive on feeding on demand (in the case of breastfeeding - this often works better for both mum and baby as the frequent feeds will keep mums milk supply up. This is because milk production works by supply and demand, so feeding on demand will help to establish a good milk supply and allow your baby and your body to be in sync. So it's important to know here that scheduled routine feeds can sometimes interrupt the natural process of milk production.

It's also important to know here, that babies suck for reasons other than just to feed.

With breastfeeding in particular, babies suck to feel safe, to calm down, to cuddle and to fall asleep. This 'comfort sucking' is baby using the breast/ bottle pretty much as a dummy. Having said that - in the early days, this 'comfort sucking' can increase and maintain milk supply.

To know if baby is 'comfort sucking' instead of full on feeding - it's pretty easy if bottle feeding. If hardly any formula is being taken and instead, they just suck lightly and then stop, and repeat, this is comfort feeding.

With breastfeeding, observe your baby at the breast. Babies often make small noises when they swallow, like a little clicking or a light sigh. When the underside of your baby's chin drops down long, slow and deep like a bullfrog's throat, that's a swallow. If the movement is short, quick and shallow, it's a suck.

Sometimes comfort nursing is portrayed negatively - especially if it's to get baby to fall asleep, but I think it's totally up to you as a parent. If baby is comforted by you instead of a dummy - and if you don't mind it, then it's totally fine.

I'll be honest here, you'll end up with baby permanently attached to you, which is fine in those early weeks, but as time moves on it's helpful for you both to deferential between the comforting and the actual feeding to establish a routine. Life does indeed go on after having a baby, and while watching TV all day might be wonderful the first time around - if you have other little ones to consider this time, the continuous sucking won't be helpful for you or them.

My two little ones loved comfort sucking. My daughter had a dummy from the first few weeks and it really helped her to settle with her reflux. We ditched it around 12 moths old.

My son however, totally rejected dummies in favour of his thumb which he still sucks! (He's 9 now and there's still no getting that thumb away, but I'm not worried - as it's not *aggressive* sucking and he only uses it to to fall asleep! He SO won't thank me for adding this to my book.) I must say here that if you are breastfeeding it is best to wait at least 4 weeks or until breastfeeding is established before introducing a dummy as it can *sometimes* confuse breastfed babies.

Making an informed choice

It is important to me that parents make decisions about their own baby. Only you who can decide what is best for you and your baby. You know your own body, your own baby and you will encounter advice from midwifes, health visitors, parenting advisers, family, friends and other parents, but ultimately it is you as a parent that knows your baby and what is best for them. trust your instincts.

I'm very much a 'live and let live' parent and professional. I don't judge others on their parenting methods, just as I'd not liked to be judged by my own. I have been known regularly to stand up for the formula feeding parent who has been brow beaten by a hardy midwife, but equally I have stood up for the breastfeeding mother who has been asked to leave a cafe for feeding her child in a public place. Parenting is about choice, experience and finding out what works for you.

In my experiences both as a mother and a professional, I feel that babies thrive on routine, be it 2 hourly, 3 or 4 hourly feeds. Some babies naturally fall into a 4 hour routine (my two did) and some will want to snack every now and then and have a bigger feed every few hours. Every baby is different.

For me, this is when feeding on demand can get tricky. Feeding your baby every time they cry rather than soothing them because, perhaps they just have trapped wind, or are unsettled for another reason, can cause problems for both of you. You are stressed because they won't feed – they won't feed because they are windy or have soiled their nappy or are too hot or too cold, and there are tears all round. This makes having scheduled feeding times much more helpful.

Following a routine doesn't have to be a scary regimented routine. A flexible eating and sleeping schedule can be super-helpful if you have older children, are returning to work early, are a single parent, or just actually feel better in a routine yourself.

A flexible routine means if little one is hungry before the 'scheduled' feeding time, you can try distracting techniques and soothing and cuddles, but if baby is distressed and obviously hungry - respond promptly and forget times. The same once you introduced regular nap and bedtimes. If they are absolutely exhausted - you're not going to try and keep baby awake at 12.25pm if their nap isn't due until 12.45pm! It's a bit of common sense, listening for cues, mixed with trust your instincts!

My Fi's Four for happiness routine is aimed at parents wanting to follow a feeding routine, not babies fed on demand. However - it can be adapted to suit your needs. You can follow other parts of the schedule with a feed-on-demand little one, but bear in mind it will take a little longer to leave the *wide Awake Baby Club.'*

The 'Four for happiness' routine

I based my 'four for Happiness routine on on hours that can be easily adapted to suit your life. These hours mean only (ideally) one wake-up during the night for dream feeds and work perfectly with parents who already have another child and have nursery or school runs, or work schedules to fit into their day.

Remember - this is just a guide and you can swap the hours to what will work better for you and your family as close to the four hours as possible.

6 am feed	10 am feed	2 pm feed	6 pm feed

Newborn sleep patterns: Newborns will sleep on and off with very little wakeful time in those early days and weeks. They will sleep on and off throughout the day and night. It can be helpful to have a pattern, but you can always change the routine to suit your needs as the weeks go by.

Nappy changes: Into this routine you'll need to incorporate the daily nappy changes. Every baby is different, so rather than going by a specific time (although this can help) check your little ones nappy regularly. Some babies can need changing up to 10 times a day, others around 6 to 8. The older your baby gets the less the changes BUT always change your baby if they are wet, even if they are wearing the super-duper dry clever nappies. Always change as soon as possible after a poo as your baby's skin is very sensitive and nappy rash is something you really want to avoid.

Activities: In the early days you'll likely not venture very far, but as the weeks go by it is brilliant if you can incorporate some activity into the routine. If you look in the 'Baby Play Club' chapter - there's lots of ideas for activities and places to go, incising tips on finding the right baby class should you wish to try one. Not only is this great for you - but its really aids better bedtimes for your little one.

Looking after yourself too! Between feeds ensure you eat meals and snacks too - your baby needs you to be happy and healthy, so don't be tempted to skip meals. Also ensure throughout the day you are keeping hydrated - especially if you are breastfeeding.

When dehydrated, the fluid loss causes a drop in blood volume making the heart have to work harder in order to push oxygen and nutrients through the bloodstream to the brain, skin, and muscles. This in turn can make you feel tired even when you're rested, so keep drinking water!

The 'Four for happiness' routine

6 am breast/bottle feed

After the feed, wind your baby well. I aways say 2-3 burps is a good wind! There's a section on winding techniques in the previous *Windy Baby Club'* Chapter. After winding, settle baby and let them go back to a milk-happy sleep.

Now here is your own routine choice; You can either get up before the 10am feed to get showered and dressed before your baby wakes, or stay in bed. If you are a brand new parent - I'd honestly say stay in bed! You need rest to adjust to these new night-time wake-ups.

10 am - breast/bottle feed

You may have already had baby dressed by this time dependent on how long they/you slept for. If not, after feeding and winding baby - change their nappy, wash their little face with cotton wool and water. Wash their little hands and in-between their fingers and dress them. Get up and ready for the day. If you've chosen to sleep in until now, go grab yourself a shower - it'll honestly help you feel better for the day ahead. If you have a moveable crib or baby chair, bring it to the bathroom door with you so you feel better about hearing baby if they need you.

Get out and about for a walk or meet friends afterwards!
Newborns will usually sleep again after this feed, but as your baby grows – after this feed is the perfect time for getting out and about for a walk, going to a baby group or class, or catching up with friends.

I can't stress enough how important it is to get out and about with your little one. Not in the very early days – you'll still be finding your feet as a new parent, but as the days turn into weeks, it's important to go out everyday if you can, even if it's just half an hours walk around the block just for a change of scenery.

2pm - breast/bottle feed

After this feed, wind and change baby, then settle them for *naps. Newborns of course nap on and off all day, but it's great after a couple of weeks, to get your baby settled into their crib for an afternoon nap if you can.

The reason behind this, is later on when they are older, they will have an afternoon nap after their lunch. If they nap in their cot from the very beginning, then they'll associate cot with sleep – perfect for happy bedtimes, and creating a good bedtime routine when older.

Use this time to rest yourself. Even if it's just half an hour power nap it'll really help you feel so much better and able to cope with the night feeds.

*Let baby sleep. When they wake, take them out of their crib/cot and do a nappy change. When your baby is older they'll sleep less and less in the afternoon and a more established sleep routine can be set.

When your baby is very tiny, you'll find they sleep around these times. As they get older you can incorporate play for wakeful time. There's more on playing with your baby the 'Baby Play Club' chapter.

4 pm nappy change

Aim to start bath time around 5.30 pm ready for the 6pm bedtime feed. I know this sounds super early - but bath rimes are a lovely calming way to unwind the day and get little ones into that sleepy state for bed.

You don't need to bath your baby every night, infant 2-3 times a week with top and tail washes in-between is fine.

If however, like my two - your baby loves baths, then daily is fine.

Aim to have little one ready in their nightwear and snuggled up ready for the 6pm bedtime feed.

6 pm -breast/bottle feed

Ensuring your baby has had a good feed before they go bed is a great routine to get into. What's even more important is that baby has been winded properly. This is especially important at bedtimes or nap times as trapped wind means an unsettled bedtime baby.

After this feed it's officially little one's bedtime!

Very little babies will have been most likely sleeping most of the day, but it's a really great routine to get into if you pop them to 'bedtime mode' after this feed.

It's easier and safer to have them downstairs with you in the early weeks but as time progresses - getting them sleeping in their crib or cot is ideal for crating that 'bedtime feel.' It's a great way of them getting used to 'cot means sleep time.'

Please remember - When baby is out of sight, for safety purposes always use a good baby monitor. There is more on this in 'The Better Bedroom Brigade' chapter.

10 pm - breast/bottle feed

We call this a 'dream feed.' A dream feed is when your baby is in bed or fast asleep in bedtime mode, and you are feeding them while they are sleepy or half-awake.

As the weeks pass by - it is is best if you feed in the room where they sleep, and avoid putting any bright lights on.

Try not to interact with 'cooing' noises or loud sounds as this will stimulate your baby into a more wakeful

Try leaving a landing light on to provide enough light in the room to see what you are doing but not too bright to wake baby fully.

2am - breast/bottle feed

Again, this is a dream feed. Your baby will be half-waking for a feed, but won't be fully awake. This time - feed in the room where they sleep and again, avoid putting any bright lights on. It's important to mention here that baby should ideally sleep in the same room as you for the first 6 months.

You'll most likely be half asleep yourself here, so it's important I mention that if you are feeding in bed, to try and avoid falling asleep fully as hard as this may be. (If you are co-sleeping - please read my safe sleeping part of the the 'Cool Crib' chapter!)

Sometimes this feed can feel like the loneliest feed - and so I set up a little #NightFeed hashtag many years ago for wide awake parents to chat online while feeding their little ones. It's got quite a lot of farmers and their lambs on it too now - so that always makes for cute viewing in spring in the UK early hours!

After the feed - wind, soothe and back into crib/cot for the rest of the night to sleep. sometimes little ones get a little unsettled after this feed for a variety of reasons. Check the 'Counting Sheep Brigade' chapter for tips and techniques for an unsettled baby.

That's it!

The very basic write up of the 'four for Happiness' routine. It's easy to follow, easy to adapt, but also easy to fall out of, and if you do - it really doesn't matter. Life is full of complications and interruptions and so, if you do fall out of the routine, gently get back into it day by day.

Please, please remember here - that from birth, in those precious early days, this routine can be a little more relaxed. Babies feed in shorter spells - and aiming for every 3 hours is more achievable. It's hard enough adapting to parenting without following rigid routines and you need to find your feet. Only attempt a routine if you feel you and your little one are ready.

Go by your baby, just keep the routine in the back of your mind to move towards, as routine is the magic key to a happy bedtime and happy sleep.

Cutting the 2am feed

Lot's of parents ask me (whatever routine they're in) when they can drop the early hours feed. This is entirely dependent on age and your own child. Every baby is different. Some may cut the 2am feed white early on around 6 weeks old, and some will still need a 2am or middle of the night feed for quite some time.

When your baby naturally stops waking for a feed around 2am and rarely finishes or takes the 'dream feeds' you can drop it! Oh yes - the glorious sleep shall return! (for some of you!) Please Don't drop this feed until your baby is ready. (You'll know this if they stop waking for the feed and you have to wake them for it, then after a week of doing so, you can drop the feed.)

Out of all the families I've worked with and who followed my routines *85% had stopped waking for their 2am feed around 10 weeks old when in my 'Four for happiness' routine, and almost all had stopped waking by 15 weeks old. (My own two stopped waking for their 2am feed around 7 weeks old.)

It's funny looking back to the dream-feed days as I write this on UK lockdown, with my two doing their google classroom lessons age 9 and 10 now! I miss those night feeds, those quiet snuggles while the rest of the world slept. The social media chats with other wide awake baby club members, BUT I was so glad to get a full night's sleep once the 2am feeds dropped, and I do love my sleep.

This routine can be followed until weaning begins (usually between 5 - 6 months depending on how hungry you find your baby to be or if your baby was born prematurely or not - in which case, never before 17 weeks.)

Weaning

Weaning is a very important part of your baby's development and is a great chance for your baby to explore new flavours and **start** enjoying a variety of different foods together. As it's a very personal thing - I haven't included a weaning chapter in this book. I feel weaning is a very individual process and has changed so much in the 27 years I have been working with little ones, so i always ask parents to do their own weaning based research and do what works for them.

In my last book I did include a weaning plan - but I do feel, looking back, that these kind of schedules put so much pressure on parents. Especially new parents - and it's why I've not included any here. I'm not afraid to say my methods and ideas evolve. In fact I'm proud that my methods change over time as it shows I'm constantly listening and researching so I can help parents in the best way possible - which is supporting their decision making and helping them to trust their instincts.

Some parents follow a strict weaning schedule, and some opt for baby-lead weaning. Some mix it up a bit. Whatever your choices I've put some great weaning resources in the back of this guide for you to have little look at.

When weaning is established, the times of the daily routine are changed to fit in with breakfast, lunch and dinner.

Usually, little ones will have a nap not long after breakfast, then a longer nap after lunch. there's more on this in the napping section and bedtime routines coming up in a bit.

How do I stick to the routine when my baby is unsettled?

If you want to follow a routine, and if you want it to work - consistency is key here, and it is important to stick to your routine as closely as possible or it won't work. Having said this, sometimes babies go through growth spurts, (*more about this in Chapter Five: The Counting Sheep Brigade*) illness, teething and for one reason or another are a little out of sink. Sticking to the routine will help them, but might not be possible - so please don't go worrying if you go off track for whatever reason. You can always come back to it when things have settled down.

Times when routine goes out of the window!

When your little one is unusually unsettled and you just have to ride the wide-awake baby club wave until everything is back to normal.

Those times may include:

• **When your baby is poorly:** It's so important if you suspect your baby is poorly not to follow sleep guides, or any sleep training you are following. A poorly baby will more than likely result in a sleepless nights until they are feeling much better. There is lots of advice in 'Wide Awake Poorly Baby Club' chapter for these times.

• **When your baby is hungry:** Remember as your baby grows they will often become hungrier, especially during the night as they have growth spurts.

If you are breastfeeding you'll most likely find your milk naturally accommodates your baby's hunger, if your baby is formula fed - you'll need to check the guide for age, and increase accordingly. If your baby is approaching the weaning months – it may be a sign to start introducing solid food.

• **When your baby is teething** Teething really sucks. As a mum to two little ones born less than a year apart - I've been walking the floor with two babies who were teething at the same time (That took some juggling let me tell you! Multiple birth parents - I salute you!) There are a few things you can do to help your teething little one and these tips are in the 'Wide Awake Poorly Baby Club' section.

What if I don't want to follow a routine?

Routine really is the magic key - but it doesn't mean you have to follow this *exact* routine. I've just shared these times as they have helped so many families over the years, and time-wise - it seems to be the best plan.

It may be that your baby is with different people on different days. Maybe you work part-time and baby goes to a nursery or childminder. If you can get everyone who is involved in the care of your baby on the same page - it really will make a huge difference if everyone try to follow a similar pattern. Consistency is key here.

Remember - you can still have a routine without the feeding schedule - it doesn't need to be regimented. As long as you have daily activities that you follow each day in a regular pattern - your little one will soon become accustomed to what is coming next. They'll recognise the daily pattern of getting up and dressed, morning walks, afternoon naps and eventually, as they start weaning - regular mealtimes.

Please don't feel in order to get great sleep you need to follow a timed schedule - routine is the magic key in whatever format you choose. The times in my schedule are jut a guide. The most important thing you can do -

is be consistent with the BEDTIME and nap routine. There's more on this in the next chapter.

Remember what I said in the introduction? *'every child is different and every family is different!'* - it's true! What works for one family may not for another and it is parents who know their children best. YOU are your little ones expert! Find a daily routine that works for you and your family, that fits in with your life and be consistent with that routine, and you'll be on your way to a happier bedtime!

Even if your daytime routine is all over the place - You may feel ready to introduce a bedtime routine when your baby is around 3 months old.

Getting your little one into a simple, calm, and happy bedtime routine can be helpful for everyone and help prevent sleeping problems later on. It's also a great opportunity to have one-to-one time with your baby.

A happy bedtime routine

In those early weeks, the days blend into nights and your newborn will sleep a lot! Even during these times, rom as early as two weeks old, you can begin to show your little one the difference between night and day and get into good routine habits.

In the daytime, when your baby is more alert:

- Wash your baby and get them dressed out of their nightwear to signal it is the start of the day.

- Make daytime feeds a little more interactive! Talk as you feed, sing or have some sound on in the background so it's not silent.

- Make sure there's lots of light - go out for walks to get some fresh air

- Make your home a silent-free zone! get baby used to normal daily noises like the vacuum or washing machine on or music in the background.

At night-time when your baby is more sleepy:

- After a wash or bath - Change your baby into nightwear to signal the beginning of bedtime and show it's the end of the day.

- During feeding - remain quiet and keep noise in your home low (not silent - or you'll be forever tiptoeing around!)

- Keep lights low/close curtains or blinds

- Swaddle to make baby feel secure and comfortable

These simple measures start the recognition between night and day and prepare for a bedtime routine as baby grows.

From around 6 weeks, your baby starts to develop their natural circadian rhythms, which is the process that helps regulate the sleep-wake cycle. Around this age you can start to introduce a bedtime routine, but it might be a little soon to be putting them to bed in another room just yet. In the first few months - it is best if they are with you until you go to bed.

However, this doesn't work for everyone. so, if you are watching TV and they are going to bed - it's important you use a baby monitor to hear them and know they are safe.

If baby is staying up with you until you go to bed - get them into a good bedtime habit by putting them into a quiet part of the room that is darker. It doesn't have to be silent - you can still watch TV, but have baby settled to sleep in their own space to get them used to the idea it's bedtime. when you go up to bed - try and keep quiet and avoid coin or chatting to them as you transfer them to their night-time sleep space. For the first 6 months it is also recommended that your baby sleep in the same room as you if possible.

This gentle guidance will prepare them for when you are ready to start a proper bedtime routine.

A happy bedtime

I can't begin to tell you the importance of a regular, *happy*, bedtime routine. It really is essential to a good nights sleep. A bedtime without tears is a much nicer bedtime for everyone involved. Nobody wants tears at bedtime, nobody wants to hate the end of the day and dread putting a child to bed, so make the effort for a brilliant bedtime routine as a baby and you'll all be on your way to better nights throughout childhood.

It goes without saying really, that daily routines combined with brilliant bedtime routines work best of all - but as I've said previously, every family is different, and sometimes a daily routine that is more regimented - just won't work for some families.

When it comes to bedtime - find something that works for you and stick to it. I'm going to share an *ideal* bedtime routine, and then show how you can adapt it to your life.

Make bedtime a good time, not rushed. Many parents, when tired, crave their little ones bedtime and rush it all too quickly, so the magical bonding time of the bedtime hour is lost. This might work now - but in the toddler and primary school years that follow - you'll end up with children that just won't settle.

I love the quietness of bedtime with my little ones after the busy days. The time to reconnect and catch up. The stories, the chat about our day, when they were babies, the quiet bedtime feed and cuddles after their bath. The smell of their baby hair and the sound of them feeding before sleep is something I will always treasure.

Taking the time at bedtime - meant I always put them into their cot awake, letting them slowly drift off in that sleepy state, knowing they were happy. No need for tears, no stress, just happy bedtimes. It was the same with all the little ones in my care. I'd often do bedtimes in my role as a professional Nanny, and I always took the time to do it properly - even when I'd already sometimes done an 11 hour shift and felt tired.

They are much the same now, only after our bedtime chats - they read before falling asleep. It's that important routine they are so used to, that has given them the gift of a happy bedtime from birth right up to their primary school years now.

Establishing a happy bedtime routine

You may feel ready to introduce a bedtime routine when your baby is around 3 months old. Getting them into a simple, soothing bedtime routine can be helpful for everyone and help prevent sleeping problems later on.

when it comes to the place of your baby's sleep - take a look at 'Chapter Twelve: The Cool Crib Brigade - Creating a safe and comfortable sleep space for baby.'

The ideal routine consists of:

- Evening bath or wash and fresh nappy

- Changing into nightwear

- Dimming the lights or using a night-light in the bedroom to create a calm atmosphere

- Snuggling up for a feed (but ideally not falling asleep during this feed)

- Singing a lullaby or having a story (never too little for a bedtime story!)

- Make baby feel secure and comfortable (use a baby sleep bag or swaddle depending on your own informed choice.)

- Into bed with white noise, a musical box nearby out of reach, the gentle hum of the TV downstairs/in another room or silence if you prefer.

This routine should take around an hour so aim to start the bedtime routine around 5.30pm with an aim for baby to be in bed by 6.30pm. Again - this is just a suggestion. Sometimes the routine may take longer. Choose a time that works for you but remember - an overtired baby, is a grouchy and unsettled baby, and this will make settling to sleep a little more tricky.

Should I swaddle my baby?

Parents have been swaddling newborn babies for centuries and it definitely has its benefits. But it also has its risks and drawbacks, too. Like all things parenting - choosing to swaddle your baby is about making an informed choice. (I know I keep saying this - but it is so important!)

This book is full of tips, techniques and ideas based on research, experiences, qualifications and training, I share the thoughts behind the techniques for you to then make a choice. You know your baby better than me - *you* are your baby's best expert. I am just here to advise and share my ideas with you.

Swaddling has been around for many years - is a traditional practice of wrapping a baby up gently in a light, breathable blanket to help them feel calm and sleep. They should only have their body wrapped and not their neck or head. The whole idea behind swaddling nowadays - is that being swaddled will help your little one feel snug and secure, like how they felt in the womb.

Many have presumed that swaddling was invented in the Palaeolithic period, but the earliest recorded depictions of swaddled babies are votive offerings from Crete and Cyprus, 4000 to 4500 years old.

During Tudor times, swaddling involved wrapping the new baby in linen bands from head to foot to ensure the baby would grow up without physical deformity. A stay band would be attached to the forehead and the shoulders to secure the head. Babies would be swaddled like this until about 8 or 9 months old!

The Swiss surgeon Felix Würtz (approx 1500-1598) was the first who criticised aspects of swaddling openly.

In the seventeenth century, the scientific opinion towards swaddling began to change. There was an association of neglect with swaddling, especially regarding wet-nurses who would leave babies in their care swaddled for long periods without washing or comforting them.

More than a hundred years after Würtz, physicians and philosophers from England began to openly criticise swaddling and finally demanded its complete abolishment. The British philosopher John Locke (1632–1704) rejected swaddling in his 1693 publication *Some Thoughts Concerning Education*, becoming a lobbyist for not binding babies at all. This thought was very controversial during the time, but slowly gained ground, first in England and later elsewhere in Western Europe.

Today, medical and psychological opinion on the effects of swaddling is divided. Some modern medical studies indicate that swaddling helps babies fall asleep and to remain asleep for longer, helps to keep the baby in a supine position, which lowers the risk of sudden infant death syndrome (SIDS,) and can soothe a fractious and unsettled baby. Other studies suggest that swaddling may interfere with the beginning breast-feeding (babies use their hands to feed and feel around not just their hands,) can increase the risk of hyperthermia, and additionally emerging evidence is showing that certain swaddling techniques may increase the risk of developmental dysplasia of the hip.

The American Academy of Pediatrics (AAP) also suggested that the decreased arousal that makes it harder for the baby to wake up, can be a problem and potentially be one of the reasons that babies die of SIDS. While this all seems alarming and overwhelming information - it is important to include both sides of the opinion when it comes to swaddling so you can make an informed choice.

Further research opportunities are logged at the back of this book should you with to investigate further.

If you do decide to swaddle your baby - here are some ways you can do it safely.

Back to Sleep: To reduce the risk of SIDS, it's important to place your baby to sleep on their back, every time you put them to sleep. This is even more important if your baby is swaddled. Some studies have shown an increased risk of SIDS and accidental suffocation when babies are swaddled if they are placed on their stomach to sleep, or if they roll onto their stomach as they can't move themselves or lift their heads when their arms are swaddled.

With this in mind, parents should stop swaddling as soon as their baby shows any signs of trying to roll over. (Many babies start working on rolling at around 2 months of age.)

The emptier the cot - the safer the sleep: Don't have any loose blankets in your baby's crib or cot. A loose blanket, cuddly toys or cot bumpers could cover your baby's face and increase the risk of suffocation.

Cot to sleep: Your baby is safest in their own crib or bassinet, not in your bed. Especially when swaddled.

Keep Hips Loose: Babies who are swaddled too tightly may develop a problem with their hips. Studies have found that straightening and tightly wrapping a baby's legs can lead to hip dislocation or hip dysplasia, an abnormal formation of the hip joint where the top of the thigh bone is not held firmly in the socket of the hip. Opt for hip-healthy swaddling" which allows baby's legs to bend up and out rather than being restricted.

Keep cool: Use light and soft and stretchy fabrics or purpose-made light swaddles instead of blankets to reduce the risk of hyperthermia.

Regularly monitor your baby: Check that baby is OK when swaddled - use a video camera monitor if possible, or tiptoe in every now and then to check baby is OK and hasn't rolled over.

When done correctly, swaddling can be an effective technique to help calm infants and promote sleep, but if you plan to swaddle your little one please make sure you are doing it safely.

Daytime naps

Daytime naps are pretty much part of your little ones life for the first 2.5 - 3 years.

Newborn nappers: In the early days, babies sleep so much and so irregularly that they don't really need to nap. In the very early weeks your baby's napping is a very much 'sleep when I want to' plan. The National sleep foundation found that (on average) newborns sleep from 10 to 18 hours per day, for periods lasting anywhere from 20 minutes to 3 hours. Many babies sleep most of the day and then are active at night – so don't worry about setting a rigid nap time routine from day one, as it just won't work. Sleep is needed for growth – which is why your little bundle of loveliness sleeps so much, only waking to feed before dozing off again for another sleep. Having said this, you can, of course, teach your little one the difference between night and day as they don't come into this world knowing which is which!

Teach the difference between night and day: To teach your little one the difference between night and day keep daytimes bright, light and noisier than the nights would be. Have background music on, talk in a normal volume, and do the things you'd normally do during the day.

At night-time – do the opposite! Make things darker, calmer and quieter. Talk in a lower voice, although don't whisper as baby will always need to sleep in the total peace and quiet! Use black out blinds in summer months, and keep things cosy and calm. These simple tricks help your baby to understand the difference between night and day and eventually will help you start a great routine.

Make nap time, a nice (non-stimulating) time! Often babies don't want to nap because there are far more interesting things to do. It's the old FMO - that keeps them from their daytime slumber, so ensure the bedroom or place of their nap is a nice, calm and comfortable place to sleep, then they'll be more likely to settle. Make the room darker using black out blinds or close the curtains. Make sure they are warm/cool enough and in older babies who have progressed up to clothes from one-pieces, take off any trousers or tights that might make napping uncomfortable.

ensure nappy is fresh and dry, tummy is full, and give your little one their favourite comforter and settle them down to sleep.

Wind down time!

In older babies as they have more wakeful time (from around 5 months) As nap time approaches - make everything calmer and quieter. Get your little one in the napping zone! Babies can benefit from a baby massage which is perfect for relaxing before a nap! There's a popular, easy-to-follow tutorial on my YouTube Channel if you'd like to have a try of this.

Keep conversation to a minimum: As hard as it is not to coo and baby talk to your little bundle – keep the chat to a minimum as any stimulation can cause a sleepy baby to go into full wake up mode. Stick with simple sentences like 'It's sleepy time now, settle down for naps' or a simple Shh-shh, then pop them into their place of sleep and stroke their head for a minute to settle.

Routine is the magic key! Having the same nap routine each day can create a wonderful napper. For babies under 12 months, from around 5 months, aim for a short morning nap of up to an hour (between 8-10) and a longer afternoon nap of up to 2 1/2 hours (between 12.30-330) for perfect napping!

It's important to mention here that napping after 4pm can cause problems with the nighttime bedtime routine as it's too close to night-time hours. (Most babies go to bed around 630/7pm)

Naps don't need to always be at home! Naps on the go are fine and often essential if you don't want to be controlled by the routine. Investing in a good black out SAFE sleeping cover like the *Snoozeshade*, is great for naps when out and about. Car naps are fine – but if your little one does fall asleep in their car-seat and you then arrive home, transfer them into their crib or cot for safe sleeping. Little ones shouldn't be in carseats for log periods of time.

Also remember if you come in from outdoors and your little one is sleeping happily lying down in their pram, to remove any covers/hats and foot-muffs to avoid overheating. Ideally you should transfer them to their crib or cot too but I know this can be hard to achieve without waking them!

If you are outside and bay is napping in their pram near you - ensure they are in the shade and don't be tempted to put a blanket over the top for shade - this can raise the temperature inside the pram area and be very dangerous. Invest instead in a safe pram shade or cover.

By investing time to create good naps during the day - in time, it'll really benefit the evening bedtime routine and sleep.

What if my baby won't settle?

There are many reasons why your baby might not settle - and you have to become a 'baby detective' to work out what is wrong.

In the next two chapters we look at why your baby may be crying, recognising the different cries and tips for settling them. The next chapter *The Windy Baby Club - Simple solutions for settling* looks at the most common reason for an unsettled baby: Trapped wind!

CHAPTER SIX: THE WINDY BABY CLUB - SIMPLE SOLUTIONS FOR SETTLING

Every parent knows a windy baby is a grumpy baby! Your baby's digestive system can give you endless worries in the early days, but there is a way to work out what's making them uncomfortable - and how to get them happy again.

Causes of trapped wind in babies

Wind is caused by excess air getting trapped in the tummy and often occurs when your baby accidentally swallows mouthfuls of air when feeding or gulps it in while crying. It is common from the newborn stage to about 3 months, as their little digestive system matures and can make your little one feel full even if they haven't actually had enough to eat.

Symptoms of trapped wind: If your baby gets air trapped in their tummy, they'll feel uncomfortable and unable to settle. Common signs your baby has trapped wind include squirming or crying during a feed or looking pained or uncomfortable when you put them down afterwards.

It can take time and patience to soothe a windy baby and dislodge the wind, but after every feed, you should ensure you get 3-4 big burps. You can do this in several ways but it's really about finding out what works for you and your baby.

How to wind your baby

There are several different ways to wind your little one, some are more common than others, but I've used all of these techniques over the years with babies in my care and on my own town title ones. Get the technique right and it could provide instant relief for your little one (and elevate the worry for you!)

• **The classic rub:** Sit your baby on your lap facing to the side or facing forward. Support your baby with one arm under their tummy and your hand supporting the chin. Lean baby forward slightly and rub the back up and down quite quickly with your free hand.

• **Pat-a-back:** Gently pat your baby's back while they are sitting in the position mentioned above. Patting can help to dislodge stubborn wind, but be careful not to pat your baby too hard!

• **The gentle under-arm lift:** One of the best ways of helping my little ones stubborn wind was to lift them gently under their arms then rock them very gently side to side, so their legs are dangling and free. This really helps to shift wind and is especially great for reflux. Only use this technique if you feel confident to do so and ensure you're careful to support your baby's head while doing so.

• **Tummy-time burping:** Lay your baby tummy-down on your lap supporting their head with your hand, or on the floor on a blanket with head to the side.

Ensure baby is safe and secure and not in danger of rolling off your lap - then use your free hand to rub the back gently up and down or in circular motions. Lots of little ones like this technique but be warned - it can bring up a sicky-burp after a feed as there is pressure on their tummy.

• **Baby massage:** Massage is a great baby calmer and can help your bond to grow stronger. What's more, it's pretty easy once you know what to do. Your newborn will be in the mood for a massage around 45 minutes after a nap and feed.

As you build confidence, try 'soothing strokes', where you move your hands from just above baby's belly button towards the hips, one after the other, to help move wind through the bowel.

A baby massage is a great way of soothing your little one and dislodging their wind and there's a really easy-to-follow tutorial on my YouTube channel.

• **Medicines:** Some medicines, like Infacol are also hugely helpful if given to your baby before a feed. It helps your little one bring up their wind by making their wind bubbles bigger and therefore easier to pass. Always read the label and follow instructions carefully if using these ind of colic medicines.

Baby still uncomfortable?

If your little one's stubborn wind is still leaving you wanting to tear your hair out, there are plenty of other tricks you can try.

1. Elevating the head end of the cot when putting your baby down for a nap after a feed can really help windy babies or those with reflux.

2. Winding during, as opposed to after, a feed (especially for bottle-fed babies) can help as well. Sit them upright half way through a feed and try to burp them, then continue to feed, however, if your baby's feeding well and seems happy, don't stop to wind as they might get upset and gulp in air as they cry!

3. If you are bottle feeding - try to use anti-colic bottles. (As your baby feeds, the valve that is integrated into the nipple flexes of an anti-colic bottle, allows air into the bottle to prevent vacuum build up and vents the air to the back of the bottle. It keeps air in the bottle away from the baby's tummy to help reduce wind.)

4. Walk around with baby upright close to your chest, head rested on your shoulder. The moment is often enough to dislodge any trapped wind.

As a parent myself, I have spent many nights walking the floors with a windy baby as sometimes it is the only thing that settles them. My husband had a rather wonderful technique of walking while 'bopping up and down' and humming the rift to *'Come as you are'* by Nirvana. It worked a treat.

Winding a fractious baby can be very stressful - especially if it takes a long time to shift the wind. If you find yourself getting really stressed, pop baby down and take a few moments to compose yourself before trying again. We all have times of feeling totally overwhelmed, so don't feel like a failure or be too hard on yourself if you need a moment to compose yourself.

Try putting some soothing music on in the background to take your mind off the crying. Remember babies cry to communicate - so think of it as your baby *telling you* they are uncomfortable - chat to them as if you understand, use a calming voice or sing and so try not to lose patience even the you are feeling really exhausted.

If wind feels like it is happening all the time and there seems to be no break - it could be reflux.

There's more on this in the next chapter.

CHAPTER SEVEN: THE REFLUX BABY CLUB - HOW TO COPE AND HELP YOUR BABY

It only feels like yesterday. In my oh-so tired arms my little boy is screaming again. His little rigid body fights my cuddles and he simply will not settle. He's 3 weeks old and fighting silent reflux.

My experience tells me to try everything - singing, talking, walking, patting, stroking, and yet nothing will pacify this little new life who is screaming louder than I thought a tiny baby could scream.

Knees raised, fists clenched, hours of crying often screaming in discomfort, I knew these familiar symptoms and took a sigh of 'oh here we go again' as I paced the room talking and singing and watching the hours pass by. Sadly, like his older sister Betsy, Oscar developed reflux after only a few weeks of life and the minute the tell-tale signs showed themselves I knew we needed medical help.

What is reflux?

Reflux is the name given when a baby regurgitates the contents of his stomach back into the oesophagus, or mouth.
Active or 'normal' reflux happens when your baby spits/sicks-up milk that has travelled back up from the tummy or in some cases, babies who have reflux swallow the milk that comes up, instead of spitting it out.

Silent reflux is when the milk starts to come up, but doesn't get as far as the mouth and there's no spit-up.

Some babies won't seem bothered by the condition, while for others, the stomach acid will burn their throat and make them uncomfortable and unsettled, and for some babies, it can cause weight loss and a 'failure to thrive.'

Babies have a tendency to reflux because:

- Babies have small stomachs.

- Babies spend a lot of their time in a lying position.

- Babies are fed mostly a fluid diet. (Milk can easily come up, particularly with a burp.)

- Handling, such as diaper changing and bouncing can increase the pressure on a baby's full tummy, which then increases the risk of spitting up. Other potential causes for reflux can include an intolerance to cow's milk protein or other allergies.

So, what happens?

Food is supposed to travel in one direction through your body, down the oesophagus, into the stomach and through the bowel. But in a child who suffers with reflux, there is a weakness in the band of muscles in the lower oesophagus. These join the stomach, acting as a valve.

If this valve doesn't shut properly, milk can travel back up, resulting in your baby vomiting (active reflux) or having a heartburn type of sensation, (silent reflux.)

The trouble for many new parents is actually recognising the symptoms and then managing to get help. So many parents struggle on, unaware their little one is suffering from the condition, and many who do try and get advice are often fobbed off by their doctors or health visitors.

Recognising the signs of reflux:

If your baby has reflux, you might notice that they regurgitate a little milk after feeding. It can also cause discomfort in their oesophagus and make them cough a little. Don't worry, as long as your baby is otherwise well and healthy, they'll be fine. You just need to keep a cloth or tissue handy for catching their milk.

In some cases, where reflux symptoms are bad, (vomiting is bad, the baby is always unsettled after feeds,) you might want to speak to your midwife, health visitor or doctor about treatment.

This is worthwhile when:

- Reflux is happening more than five times a day on a regular basis.

- Your baby cries excessively after feeds.

- Your baby vomits regularly.

- Coughing becomes a regular occurrence.

How do you treat baby reflux?

• **Try feeding your baby in an upright position for feeding if you can -** This can be quite a task if you are breastfeeding, so try lots of different positions to see what works best.

• **Take time to wind your baby -** Babies with reflux often struggle with extra wind too, so take time to ensure they've got all of their wind up after a feed. Check the previous 'Windy Baby Club' chapter for tips.

• **Try holding baby in an upright position for 20 minutes after feeds -** or try smaller but more frequent feeds.

• **Seek medical support** from your GP if your baby is in distress and you have tried everything and symptoms continue after 2 weeks. If your baby is formula-fed, you may be given a powder that's mixed with formula to thicken it a pre-thickened formula milk If the thickening powder does not help or your baby is breastfed, a GP or specialist might recommend medicines that stop your baby's stomach producing as much acid.

• **Be patient** As stressful as it can be, most babies 'spitting up' has decreased remarkably by the age of 5 or 6 months and disappears completely by the age of 12 months. Both my babies 'grew' out of their reflux when they were around 5 months old. In severe cases it may persist for up to 18 months or more.

If your baby is diagnosed with reflux, try not to worry. You're not alone in your suffering! As many as 1 in 3 babies suffer with some form of reflux in the early days and there is lots of support out there.

If you feel unable to cope - always talk to someone. If you can get help to have a break - take it! A baby with reflux is incredibly hard to cope with so ditch any parent guilt you may have about taking a break.

Chapter Eight: The Baby Detectives Club - Why is my baby crying?

If you are a brand-new parent reading this - please, please don't stress about not knowing the difference between baby cries. It is something you learn as the weeks pass, and crying babies is always a little stressful - so don't worry if you find it overwhelming - it is completely normal to feel that way.

Your baby will probably be fairly quiet and sleepy for the first couple of weeks of life. As they start to become more awake and alert, they might start to cry more, for longer periods of time until they reach three to four months old.

Before we look at the different reasons why babies cry and how to recognise certain cries, it's important to say that babies cry to communicate.

All babies cry, some a little more than others. Crying is your baby's way of telling you they need comfort, care, or something is wrong. There's a difference between the cries which you'll pick up in time, but let's look at the reasons why your baby may be crying.

Here are the most common reasons:

- Hunger
- Tiredness
- Soiled/wet nappy
- Wanting to be held
- Wind/Colic/Reflux
- Too hot or too cold
- Boredom
- Overstimulation
- Unwell
- Teething

Since your baby can't exactly tell you what they needs with words, they rely on an array of whimpers, cries and all-out screams to get your attention. It can be really hard at first to recognise the differences in those sounds and signs, so I've written them down explaining the sounds as best I can on paper!

The 'I'm really hungry' cry.

This often sounds like a low-pitched, rhythmic and repetitive cry. Ut usually comes with other signals such as sucking, lip-smacking, rooting rooting for the breast, or sucking on fingers. Although this often starts low-pitched and rhythmic, it can become faster, louder and almost unconsolable if ignored or left too late with feeding.

Respond to hunger cries quickly so your baby doesn't get too worked up - otherwise this can make feeding difficult, and can also make baby feed too fast and take in large gulps of air which in turn can cause trapped wind.

The 'I'm tired' (or uncomfortable) cry.

This cry is more like a slow, whiny, continuous cry that builds in intensity the longer baby is left. Body language includes rubbing eyes (if tired) or fidgeting and looking uncomfortable (if soiled/wet nappy.)

Check your baby's nappy regularly and change when needed. In the early days you'll be changing more frequently and the revolting early-day nappies can really irritate newborn skin if left. Keep in mind that your baby may also cry if too hot or cold - so check how you've dressed them for the weather. Too many layers? Not enough? Check and adjust if needed.

For tiredness look for the cue signs. In the early weeks your baby will sleep for lots in the daytime. For older babies - ensure they are getting regular daytime naps (look back at the sleep guidance chart for details.)

The 'I've had enough' cry

This cry is a fussy, whiny, repetitive cry getting louder and more adjusted the longer baby is ignored.

Body language includes turning their head away from any loud noises or lights that they don't like, being fidgety, and putting hands to face and ears in older babies.

When you recognise this cry, move your baby away whatever it is that is upsetting them. Try calming your little one in a calmer, quieter room or try some gentle music or white noise to soothe.

The 'I'm bored' cry

Yup - babies get bored, just like older children! It could be a change of scene is needed, or they just want your attention! This cry is usually in older babies rather than the early weeks and will start out as happy sounds, turning to into a fussing, whiny sound as time passes. This usually happens when baby has had your attention and you turn away, or an activity they were enjoying comes to an end.

If you pick your baby up or give the attention back right away and the crying stops - you'll know this is the reason why!

You can't hold your baby all the time - so if it's not possible to keep the attention going all the time because you need to pay attention to another child, or do something else important and you are sure it is because the attention has stopped, use distraction. Try a musical toy or rattle that is tactile and interesting or a change of scene or position (from playmate on the floor to a baby chair for example.)

The 'I've got wind' cry

This cry is usually loud. It is usually intense wails or screams.

Body language includes rigid body or fidgeting and baby gets hot and sweaty quickly from being upset and uncomfortable. Try some of my winding techniques in the *Windy Baby Club*' chapter.

The 'I'm not feeling very well' cry

This is often a gentle cry. More like soft whimpers that are lower in pitch. It's a proper -get-you-in-the-heart cry. This is often the cry your baby will make when they are teething - getting louder if not helped with pain relief or soothed.

If your baby is poorly - there will be other symptoms to look out for including a raise in temperature.

A normal temperature in babies and children is about 36.4C, but this can vary slightly. A high temperature or fever is usually considered to be a temperature of 38C or above.

Have a look in the 'Poorly Baby Club' chapter for more details on baby illness and how to help your little one, but always contact a GP or call 111 (UK) if:

- Your child has other signs of illness, such as a rash, as well as a high temperature

- Your baby's temperature is 38C or higher if they're under 3 months old

- Your baby's temperature is 39C or higher if they're 3 to 6 months old

Should I ever ignore my baby's cry?

There are times when you can't get to your baby right away and you really shouldn't worry or berate yourself if you can't respond right away. Babies cry to communicate a need, but as parents we are only human and cannot physically respond to *every* single whimper and cry (toilet break anyone?)

When you need to do something else

You need to have a shower, go to the loo, brush your teeth and cook meals - sometimes babies can't be held and comforted during these times - and it really won't cause any long lasting damage to let them cry while you are otherwise occupied. I'm not suggesting pouring a large glass of red, settling to watch Netflix and ignoring your baby for long periods of time here - it's about common sense.

For single parents in particular, or parents with one partner working long hours while they take on the baby care - you cannot respond to every single cry at every moment of the day unless you are super-human, or strap your baby to you while you to go to the loo. (Please don't do this!) In this respect - ignoring your baby for a moment is fine.

Tears at bedtime

There has been so much debate about the 'controlled crying' technique over the years. In my first book - I included the 'Cry it out' method - as it's also called, as so many parents came to me for how to use this method and I wanted to adapt it to make sure it was used correctly in as gentle a way as possible for both parents and baby. (I had heard stories of babies being left for long periods to cry themselves to sleep - and wanted to ensure that anyone choosing this method absolutely didn't do that.)

I chose to include this method again in this book, because I believe parenting is about making an informed choice. You can read about this technique and research for and against it, in the 'settling baby' chapter, but in short here - when used correctly, in timed intervals, not leaving baby for long periods of time, there is no research to support any long lasting damage to your baby.

When it's all too much

When it comes to babies crying - it can be incredibly stressful. As a professional I have the training and experience to deal with these stressful times, and even I fond it difficult, but for new parents, with no baby experience - it can be incredibly tough. Add to this very little sleep, and many parents really struggle to cope. *These* are the times when parents need a break.

If you really can't cope with the hours of crying and are at breaking point - please (if at home) put baby in a safe place, walk away into another room and take some deep breaths to calm down for a moment, before returning to comfort your little one and try something new. You are not failing - you are doing what is absolutely right for both your sakes.

Ideally, if you are in a partnership or have additional help at home - take it in turns to comfort little one when the crying goes on for a long time so the other person gets a much needed break.

Don't feel guilty for needing to walk away for a moment - we have all had those moments as parents and it is OK to feel overwhelmed.

Remember these times for baby crying are short, even though at the time the nights and days seem endless.

CHAPTER NINE: CH,CH,CHANGES - GETTING BACK INTO GOOD SLEEP HABITS AFTER CLOCK CHANGES AND HOLIDAYS!

There are so many ch, ch, ch, changes (sorry! Huge Bowie fan here,) that can disrupt a usual happy baby sleeper and make them become fully fledged *Wide Awake Baby Club* member!

Two of the biggest changes to effect a usually brilliant sleeper, are the clock changes and family holidays.

In the UK, the clocks go forward an hour in Spring, and back an hour in Winter and can cause chaos even with that little hour of change.
Family holidays bring their own bedtime changes and can have the happy sleeper, turn in to a *wide awake baby* in no time at all though over-tiredness and lack of routine to their days.

I love holidays. Don't we all? We all fall into holiday habits when we go away, you know the thing, the late nights and lazy mornings, and while these are wonderful and O.K for a week or two, they can cause major issues that take a while to fix.

Not only do they stop decent bedtime hours, they put the whole daytime routine out of whack and feeding schedule goes a little wonky. So how do we ensure these ch, ch, ch changes (sorry) don't make everything go wrong that we've previously worked hard to achieve?

Holidays

Decide before traveling if its worth changing your bay's schedule. If you're only taking a short trip one or two time zones away, it may be better to just keep your child on their normal sleep schedule and set meal times, naps and bedtime an hour earlier or later, depending on whether you headed east or west. For example, if you traveled somewhere that's an hour ahead, baby's standard 5pm teatime simply happens at 6 pm local time and bedtime slides from 7 to 8 pm - it doesn't really matter.

On holidays it is so easy to fall out of routine. you are relaxed - having a break, and may not want to stick to the schedule. Instead of ditching the routine altogether - stick to it loosely.

If your holiday is leading to later bedtimes - don't worry! The holidays are for fun times, but you can still keep a routine in place. Stick to the same bedtime routine but just increase the stay-up time! Perhaps baby goes to bed usually at 6.30pm but you want to go out for dinner? Keep their schedule in place for feeds and take them out with you in the pram using a snooze shade or similar to keep their pram cosy and dark while out and about. This means the routine is still in place - it's just happening in a different place.

Jet lag and the wide-awake baby

I've been lucky enough to travel to far-off places in my time, and a few times with the little loves in tow. One thing I don't love about travelling is jet lag.

For adults, jet lag sucks, but what's worse is helping little ones get into the vibe of a new time zone. Nobody wants to start their holiday cranky with an unsettled baby!

With this in mind - there's a few things you can try to make jet-lag a little lighter.

Shift the body clock before you travel: Lots of my travelling parent buddies, have told me they find travelling easier when they shift their body clocks a few days before travelling long-haul to prepare in advance. Little ones circadian rhythms generally catch up with them naturally after 3 or 4 days, so it's not essential to do this before you travel, but could make it easier for babies.

Sometimes, shifting your baby's bedtime by a couple of hours toward the destination time-zone a few days before your travel can also really help.
work out feeding times before you travel to see where they are likely to fall in the new time zone and note them down.

Get into the time zone at the airport: Set your clocks to the time of your destination so you feel like you're already on that time zone. By doing this before you arrive, you are tricking yours and your baby's body into the new time zone.

If it's night-time in the place you're landing, but daytime on the plane - try and encourage a good few hours sleep on the journey there to get the body thinking it's bedtime. With babies this can be easier said than done -

so let them travel in comfortable clothes and have their favourite sleep-comfort handy so it puts them in the sleep zone frame of mind. Feeding on take-off and landing will also settle them and helps with ears popping due to cabin pressure.

Keep hydrated: Travelling dehydrates us quickly - so keep your little loves topped up, even if this means more nappy changes during the flight. I know, I know - bathroom visits on an aircraft with little ones isn't fun, but you'll all feel better for keeping hydrated!

Dehydration can add to that woozy jet-lag feeling when we land in the new time-zone, so by keeping hydrated you're all less likely to feel awful and more able to enjoy your holiday right away.

Get some sunshine: While it's important to be sun-safe (don't forget to pile on the sun-cream,) if you are arriving at what would be your little ones bedtime, get out in the sunshine and soak up the rays. Sunlight helps your body and brain make sense of the new time zone and resets your inner clock, so try and keep them awake as long as possible into the new time-zone, but don't stress if they fall asleep -they are little after all. remember to keep unsafe and protect your little ones skin, head and and eyes.

Keep nap times going: Naps are important for good night sleep - so keep up with the daily nap routine and you'll find the nights a lot easier. Put baby in the shade for naps in their pram with a snooze shade cover out of direct sunlight. Check on them regular - especially in hot countries and have naps in cool rooms if possible. Babies can overheat very quickly so let them sleep in just their nappy if out and about, but in the hotel room - ensure they don't get too cold if there is aird conditioning.

Things will get back to normal in time when the body clock adjusts, so try not to stress too much and go with the flow.

Sleeping in the heat - how to help your baby sleep on holiday and keep their cool!

In the glorious summer months or while on holiday, sleep can often become disrupted due to the heat or a change in routine. A lack of sleep added to hot summer days can result in a grumpy baby and unhappy parents which isn't a fun way to spend the summer at all!

Fan-tastic sleep! It's worth investing in a fan for the summer months as they can really make a difference to hot, muggy bedrooms.
By circulating the air in your baby's room, you're keeping them from the

risk of overheating, waking and thus helping them get a good nights sleep.

It's important to note here that if you're using a fan to be safe. Ensure it is out of baby's reach (including wires) and that it's not pointed directly at their bed so they get too cold.

Too hot to sleep? Hot sticky nights cause disrupted sleep for many adults who can re- adjust their bedclothes or pyjamas to get comfy! Babies rely on us to keep them comfortable and cool at night, so think comfort when putting your baby to bed in hot weather.

Less is best so rather than pyjamas - let them sleep in just a vest with their nappy, or just their nappy. To avoid over-heating ditch blankets and quilts and sleeping bags and don't swaddle if it is really warm.

If you want to have a window open and are at home - please consider using safety locks and make sure baby's cot isn't directly under or near the window if doing this.

If you're lucky enough to have safety windows that open a small amount and
are lockable, then these are even better. Don't be tempted to leave regular, (non-safety) windows open wide for obvious reasons.

Leave bedroom doors open, and use a fan (as mentioned above,) to circulate the air in their room - this often keeps the whole home cool in warmer months.

Dealing with clock changes

Springtime - Spring forward into a happy bedtime: When we put the clocks forward it means an hours less sleep for us (I know, I know,) but it also means an hour less for your baby too.

You can avoid problems, strops and grumpiness that early-waking brings, by getting your baby ready about a week before the clock changes. This won't work with newborns - only those in a good day and night routine already.

Simply change bedtimes to 10-15 minutes earlier each night for seven nights. This simple tip can really help make the transition smoother and the clock change tick tock along nicely.

If you're reading this with less than seven nights to prepare - don't worry, start as soon as you can, even a couple of nights before the clock-change can really help.

Autumn time - Fall back into better bedtimes: This means an extra hour of glorious sleep for most people! For us parents – not so lucky.

In the autumn - simply reverse the springtime clock change tips above.

Whereas before, in Springtime you may need black-out blinds or curtains to help sleep in the lighter evenings, you may find the new winter times are on your side. Babies often sleep better in the winter because of our dark mornings and earlier dark nights.

Finally, the the week after clock changes or any holiday, you may find your child is unsettled. Try not to worry, they'll soon settle once they get into the new time zone and back into the routine.

By sticking to your usual daily routine, and a great, regular, bedtime routine you'll soon have a happy sleeper again.

Whatever ch, ch, ch ,changes occur during your child's daily life - the sooner you get back to routine and stick with it, you'll all be back to better sleep in no time at all.

CHAPTER TEN: SEPARATION ANXIETY AND THE SLEEP DEPRIVED: TIPS FOR CALMING, SETTLING AND COPING

Just like us grown-ups, baby's can feel worried and anxious at times too. From as young as 8 months old, a child can show anxiety in the form of *separation anxiety*. This anxiety is where little ones they become clingy and really upset when separated from their parents.

This anxiety is a totally normal stage of development and they grow it of it, usually around 3 years old.

Why separation anxiety happens

Separation anxiety refers to a developmental milestone that occurs in most babies around 6 months old. it's a sign your baby now realises how dependent they are on the people who care for them. This can include grandparents, siblings or professionals closely involved with their care, as well as you!

As they get more aware of their surroundings, your baby's strong relationship with this small group means they don't feel so safe without you. Their growing awareness of the world around them can also make them feel unsafe or worried, and new situations or with new people, even if you are there can become quite upsetting.

As worry as this sounds - it's actually a good thing! It means your little one is growing and developing and feels connected to important people in their life. Yay! The crying every time you walks out of sight? Not so 'yay!' and sometimes really stressful!

How to handle separation anxiety

Separation anxiety can make it difficult to leave your baby at nursery or in someone else's care. You may feel distressed by their tears and worry about the effect on your baby every time you need to leave them.

Remember, it's only natural for your baby to feel anxious without you as they go through this stage of development, so there's no reason to feel guilty when you need to get on with other parts of your life. There are however, things you can do to make it a little easier for you both.

Small steps: Start by leaving your baby for short moments - literally stepping out of the room (if they are safe) and talking the whole while you leave. Come back after 15 seconds, then gradually increase the time.

They will cry - and this is OK. It is a *protest* cry and them communicating with you that they don't want you to leave the room. When you return offer lots of reassurance. Build the time up that you leave (always ensuring they are safe and never letting them get distressed.)

If you are in a relationship, take time to have a half hour soak in the bath while your partner takes care of baby. Take it in turns so your baby gets used to the whole 'leaving the room' anxiety they are learning to cope with.

While teaching your little one to feel OK with your absence - always leave your baby with someone they know well so they still feel comfortable and safe while you're gone. Gradually work towards longer separations, and then, leave them in less familiar settings. It is ideal if you can do this in the run up to them starting daycare if you are returning to work, or wanting a night out uninterrupted - as it'll make the transition so much easier.

Leave a little comfort behind: It can really help your little one if you leave a little something comforting behind. Something your baby identifies with you – like a small blanket or handkerchief with your scent on it, or a favourite toy they like to sleep with. This may reassure them while you are away and make leaving a little easier for you both.

Don't worry! It's a totally normal stage of development - so please don't stress or overthink it if your little one sobs when you leave. By leaving your baby with another caregiver, you won't damage them, in fact you're actually helping them learn to cope without you, and that's an important step towards their growing independence.

How to handle separation anxiety at night

One of the many reasons a baby struggles to self-settle at bedtime, is separation anxiety.

We've looked at routine and reasons why your little one may be crying an unsettled - but if you've done everything to ensure they are comfortable - it's likely they just don't want to be without you to sleep.

This is really tough for parents - nobody likes an upset little one, and I am all for a happy bedtime with no tears if it can be helped.

These techniques are really simple and really help little ones feel reassured and calm as they drift off to sleep.

It is important to note here - that these techniques are only to settle and not to help them fall asleep. If they can settle once calmed - then this is a really brilliant step into having better nights.

By learning to 'self settle' and feel calm and happy in their sleep space - your baby will settle when they go through the light sleep phase during the night.

Rocking a tiny baby in your arms is truly wonderful, pretty special and something I encourage at any time of the day or night to settle your little one - but rocking a baby to *sleep* wont help them to learn to settle themselves. It means your little one will rely on that rocking motion every time they need to go to sleep - and without it, they will really struggle. It is the same as feeding to sleep, or stroking hair to sleep or whatever you physically do to get the to nod off.

All of these things are perfect to settle your little one and get them in the sleep state and mood for slumber - but it's not advisable to use any 'crutch' to get them to sleep.

I have many parents who have come to me for help because their now 3 year old still needs to be rocked to sleep. Now I bet these parents have sturdy backs and arms of steel - and I truly admire their dedication, but they are exhausted and their little ones can't ever settle without them.

Give your baby a chance - let your baby have the opportunity to learn to self-settle, trust them to learn, just as you will as they get older and learn to walk. You are giving them a wonderful gift - and they will thrive on it!

Putting your baby down into the crib

When you put your little one down they will make a sound and they may start to cry. Don't worry - this is normal. Babies often make sounds when they settle to sleep. In fact, the amount of noise your little one makes when they settle or indeed when they are asleep - may surprise you. These noses don't mean your baby needs picking up. Only if they are truly upset do you need to pick them up to comfort them until they are calm enough to be put back down into their crib.

Now I know many parents and some professionals use a method called control crying, also know as controlled crying, and I've touched on this briefly in previous chapters. But for me, personally, bedtime is a time for feeling calm and happy not upset and stressed. I have used it years ago before I developed my route plans and calmer techniques and it works if used correctly, but it's my least favourite method of helping little ones to self-settle.

Controlled crying technique

Control crying is a method in which you leave your baby to cry for short intervals of time and go back to check they are OK and repeat until they are quiet and settled. This is not the same as 'extinction crying' a term for letting babies 'cry it out' until they are exhausted. Do not do this – it is not appropriate at any time.

This method has had bad press in the past due to parents not following the control crying guide correctly and leaving babies to cry for long periods of time. This is something I cannot stress enough you must *NOT* do.

Parents (and some professionals) use this technique as it gets quick results. If, after conducting your own research you feel it is something you want to try, please take note - only attempt this method if:

- Your baby is older than 6 months

- You have established a good daily routine

- You have established a good bedtime routine

- Your baby is well and not showing signs of teething or discomfort

- You are confident your baby is not hungry

Stop this method if:

- Your baby becomes unwell

- You or your baby are finding this stressful

- Your baby's sleep has not improved in 2 weeks.

With this method - consistency is key. Ensure your baby is well fed, winded, is comfortable and settled into their crib or cot.

1. Kiss and snuggle your baby down into bed and say goodnight.

2. Sing a lullaby or put soothing music or white noise sounds on, and wait for a minute to see they are settled then leave the room.

3. Give your baby the opportunity to go to sleep - listen to their noises and sounds and don't go to them unless they are distressed. (Ignore any grizzles or moans - these are natural sounds babies make when they are tired and settling to sleep.)

4. If your baby starts to cry, leave them for a set period of time before returning to settle them (anything up to 3 minutes) before going back in. when return ing don't pick them up, simply place a hand on your baby and settle them. Don't turn up the lighting, and use minimal eye contact and don't coo or chat to them as this can stimulate a sleepy baby to interact and become more wakeful.

5. Keep repeating the returns and settling until baby is quiet and you are sure they are asleep. Stay close by and monitor them throughout this time.

6. If your baby is distressed at anytime and will not settle, pick them up, reassure them, calm them down, then resettle and attempt again.

This method of 'sleep training' should also be done for naps in the day too. The idea behind the retuning for brief moments is to reassure your baby you are returning. This method can take very little time to work, but it takes patience and a lot of work and effort.

Please do not leave baby crying for long periods of time. This will only add to any separation anxiety issues that may be there and make happy bedtimes unachievable in the long term.

My preferred method, and much gentler technique is my *shh-shh-pat-pat technique*.

Shh-Shh pat-pat technique

This technique can be used as soon as you start putting your little one into a bedtime routine form around 6 weeks. With this method, again, consistency is key. Ensure your baby is well fed, winded, is comfortable and settled into their crib or cot.

1.   Kiss and snuggle your baby down into bed and say goodnight.

2.   Sing a lullaby or put soothing music or white noise sounds on, and wait for a minute to see they are settle.

3.   If your baby starts to make a noise - don't worry. Simply soothe your little one with shh-ing sounds in rhythm. so, shh-shh (pause) Shh Shh (pause) and repeat. Use your hand to gently pat/tap their leg or arm or tummy. You're not doing this to get them to sleep, just to calm them and reassure them. The rhythm is soothing and calming and puts baby into a calm almost mediative state.

4.   Now move away from the cot and wait. If they stir but don't cry, leave them. If they cry, repeat the shh-shh pat-pat technique. Don't use any words, just Shh-shh-pat-pat and try to avoid eye contact, they don't need the stimuli they need to go to sleep so this means limited interaction with you. Keep repeating until they are almost asleep.

Again, this method of 'sleep training' should be done for naps in the day too.

This technique works pretty quickly and is gentle. Most of the families I work with say their little ones are settled and sleeping with very little shh-ing or patting needed towards the end of the first week.

The important thing to mention here is this method isn't designed to pat your baby to sleep because then you are just replacing rocking or other 'crutches' with patting, and you'll not thank me for a creaky back from nights of patting them to sleep over their cot!

Use this method if they wake in the night too. Don't lift them unless they are seriously distressed, wet, soiled or poorly. It's natural of course to want to do that, but in the early days of teaching self-settling, it's important to help them to settle themselves, especially in the night.

Another method you can try is my *'Bedroom bottom shuffle'* - it's as ridiculous as it sounds, but it works!

The bedroom bottom-shuffle!

This is a particularly favourite technique of mine among the parents who come to me for help. It's an even more gentle way and although it takes much longer to achieve a full nights sleep, it works well. It works with babies in cots and older children in beds too – so it's one of my favourite techniques to use throughout parenting.

With this method, again, consistency is key. Ensure your baby is well fed, winded, is comfortable and settled into their crib or cot.

1.   Kiss and snuggle your baby down into bed and say goodnight.

2.   Sing a lullaby or put soothing music or white noise sounds on, and wait for a minute to see they are settled.

3.   If your baby starts to make a noise - don't worry. It's normal for them to make little noises or whimpers as they settle. Sit by the cot of your little one quietly. Put your hand through the side of the cot bars or over the crib. you can either hold their little hand or stroke their hair.

4.   If they cry, simply shh or stroke them to settle. Don't pick baby up unless they are distressed. It is completely normal for them to make funny noises or protest groans and sounds while setting.

5.   Firstly, when your baby is quiet - let go of your little ones hand, or stop the stocking of their head, but stay by the crib.

6.   Move a little bit away from the crib by bottom shuffling away. Keep shuffling away each minute until you are near the door. It's bit like ninja parenting.

The idea behind this technique came from working when I was working I'm the early years of my career as a Professional Nanny in Greenwich, London. A 7 month old baby in my care was really unsettled at night due to illness. After a bout if chicken pox and unsettled nights - this little one was anxious to be left alone and super unsettled at bedtimes.

The reassurance of me, and then their dad sitting by their cot each bedtime, was enough reassurance to know they were safe and O.K. After only a week or so of 'bottom shuffling' away from the cot - they were able to be put down without the need of the reassurance anymore and got back into their happy bedtime routine.

With this technique you are pretty much with your baby until they fall asleep. You must however, try and avoid stroking them to sleep, but instead just 'be there' if you can.

The majority of parents who use this technique told me their babies self settle in less than 10 days and by 3 weeks they were only in the room bottom shuffling for 10 minutes! I know this sounds a long time - but I'm not about quick fixes or magic. It takes time and consistency - but that time really pays off. Theses babies weren't stroked to sleep. They simply fell asleep knowing their parent was beside them.

As the days move on, you can try sitting in the room instead of being right next to the cot and move further and further away until you are near the door and they can still see you. It is surprising (in my own experiences and those of others) how quickly this works.

Eventually you can move outside the door saying shh-shh and there is no need to stay in the room. I know this sounds like a very long-winded self-settling technique but it really works. It also is a lot easier than acing the floor night after night rocking a baby. Your back will thank me for it!

These simple but gentle techniques have proven invaluable over they years for the parents I've worked with and my own town title ones. you can mash the techniques together a bit or choose one to stick to, or if one doesn't work - try the others. It really is about finding what works for you. What works for one family, may not for another.

Consistency is key here - whatever routine and technique you use, you need to stick to it and everyone who cares for your baby needs to do them same to avoid bedtime/nap-time confusion.

CHAPTER ELEVEN: THE BABY PLAY CLUB - HOW ACTIVITIES WITH YOUR LITTLE ONE CREATES A BETTER SLEEPER!

Play is a really important part of your little ones routine and is a very important part of healthy development. Through play and curiosity, your child develops language skills, social skills such as cooperation and sharing, and physical and eventually - thinking skills such as how to do things or how things work.

In the early days your baby will be all about the feed-eat-sleep-repeat - but you can gradually introduce play and awake time into their day as the weeks go by.

Playing is one of my favourite things about being a parent. The more connections a baby makes, the better their brain will work - which is where us parents come in. It's by playing with our babies and stimulating their interest that we help shape their brain for the future. True story!

Now my two are older we get to have some fabulous fun, but I didn't wait until they were toddlers, we played together from day one in one way or another - be it singing, baby massage or lying down on the floor together looking at bright colours on blankets. Different kinds of play promote different skills. Without going full on Childhood and Youth Studies degree mode on you - it's about finding a a good mix of play that stimulates all round development.

This includes your baby's five main areas of development which are Cognitive Development, Social and Emotional Development, Speech and Language Development, Fine Motor Skill Development and Gross Motor Skill Development.

Stimulating your baby during wakeful time is essential for routine and is great for bonding. Playing with your baby helps you build a strong attachment that will give your child a safe place from which to explore the world as they grow. Responding to and playing with your baby in a caring and nurturing way will support all aspects of their healthy development.

There's no need for expensive musical soft toys or rattles in the beginning either, *YOU* are a great from of entertainment for your baby and all they really need in those early months. You are your baby's most important play thing, and they learn most from their parents in those early months. It doesn't mean you need to spend every single moment of every day entertaining your little one, but giving them plenty of your time interacting and encouraging play in the first year is super important for their development.

Playtime ideas with your baby

Forget what the baby adverts suggests you need to buy - the bright lighted toys or noisy musical boxes aren't needed in those early months of your little ones development. Here are some ideas to try.

You!

Yup! You are your baby's best toy! You're pretty awesome you know? Lay your baby down and kneel over making funny faces.

Stick your Tongue out and you might get a shock-they often do it right back at you from a very young age! Encourage tummy time and make faces, wave your fingers and hands, let them reach and touch your face and hair and lay down next to them to encourage them to roll towards you.

Repetition is important – the games you play at first probably wont achieve anything, but play peek-a-boo daily and soon you'll get a response! Try peek-a-boo with a soft scarf. Put it over your head and then reveal your face and say 'Boo!' If your baby is smiling, making noises and babbling you are doing well – if they turn away or cry, try something else. You are an entertainment machine! Make some noise, sing! Have fun!

Bright fabrics and blankets

Babies also learn through touch, so help your little one explore their world by giving them lots of different shapes and textures. Lie your baby near these so they can see the colours, let them touch crinkly material, cardboard, soft wooly scarves, furry teddy bears, wave chiffon scarves above your baby's head, and let them feel the fabrics. Remember to never leave them unattended with material or scarves that they get tangled in or suffocate under.

Books

From 0-3 months, your baby will love black and white or high contrast cloth books. They also love large images of faces!

As they get a little older, board-style baby books are great or ones they can safely chew on (babies explore with their mouths!)

Musical toys and rattles

Babies love making noise. As they get older (from around 4 months) you can introduce rattles, shakers and musical toys. you can even make your own using plastic bottles with the lids on tight filled with dried peas.
Stacking toys or blocks

From around 6 months old your baby will love playing with big blocks and stacking toys. They will take great delight in knocking over towers built by you, or if a high chair - throwing things on the floor for you to pick up again!

Soft toys

Not just for cuddling - soft toys of different textures are fabulous for your little one to explore and touch. some soft toys even have musical activities and sounds.

Activity centres
Toys that have buttons to press, levers to pull, and knobs to turn are ideal from around 7 months. Great for keeping attention and developing fine motor skills too!

Music.

My little ones adore music and have from a very young age. In fact they both kicked happily whenever I put *The Killers - Mr Brightside'* on in the kitchen hen I was pregnant with them both!

Lullabies and nursery rhymes are soothing and engaging for babies and music is even good for little ones' health. In fact, premature babies in intensive care units have been found to gain weight faster and leave the hospital sooner when they listen to 30 minutes of Mozart a day. How very clever is that?

Children love any music but babies need something a little softer than heavy metal in the early months so try some classical. Pop it on in the background, and ensure it's not too loud for sensitive little ear-drums!

Singing

Singing with your little baby is a brilliant way to support learning. One of the biggest benefits of singing is the repeated use of the 'memory muscle'. Learning a piece of information attached to a tune, embeds that information more rapidly in a child's mind.

Learn some old fashioned nursery rhymes and sing them to your baby while doing the actions. Baby will follow your hands with their eyes and later will imitate you. Join a singing group like monkey music for singing fun with other babies and parents.

Of course with everyday life it is hard to find the time to fit in lot's of activities with your baby, but remember these days fly by. Put the housework on hold and end enjoy these early days - the more you put into your baby the more you'll get back! Big wide eyes, bright smiles and gurgles all come from interaction and play. Clapping hands comes from copying and repetition.

Get out and about

Fresh air and light for baby and exercise for you, promotes a healthy appetite and sleep! It's also great for those exhausting days when you've had a bad night - it can really make you feel a million times better, even if its just a walk around the block. Make sure baby can see everything. So many parents hide their newborns snugly under hooded prams thinking it keeps them safe and warm – it does, but they're missing out on seeing the great big colourful world around them!

Baby classes

Once you have found your feet as a parent and got into a little routine - a baby class can be really beneficial for you and your little one.

There are so many benefits for little ones attending classes and groups, (including the perfect excuse for parents to get out of the house) - but finding the best activity for your little one can be pretty overwhelming! With hundreds of classes out there – it's hard to know which will suit your child best!

Choosing the right class: Like all things parenting, it's really finding what works for you and your little one and choosing something that fits in with their age and stage of development.

Music and singing classes are a brilliant way to support learning. One of the biggest benefits of singing is the repeated use of the 'memory muscle'. Learning a piece of information attached to a tune, embeds that information more rapidly in a child's mind. Dancing, swimming and even little yoga classes are fantastic for little ones physical and social development and a great way of channelling that never-ending energy.

If you really can't decide, don't worry! Many classes offer taster sessions – so it's worth trying a few before signing up for a term.

Do your research: Check the class credentials – it's something that's important and something that so many parents forget. In a recent survey by the Children's Activities Association (CAA) One of the most worrying findings was the number of parents who had assumed (incorrectly) that a Code of Practice already existed. In short – many groups and classes across the UK attended by little ones, may not have adequate child safeguarding or Health and Safety and insurance.

The CAA now have a Code of Practice that offers parents peace of mind and many popular UK classes including Water Babies, Baby Sensory, diddi dance and Tumble Tots are signed up to their list. (Check out the register at www.childrensactivitiesassociation.org.)

How to know if a class is safe and a good standard: You can start to look out for the official CAA logo on the websites and literature of all those businesses who have pledged to meet the CAA's robust guidelines for best practice.

For those not displaying the logo, don't be afraid to ask to see their insurance, CRB checks and qualification or training from all staff involved in the activities. Think about it - you wouldn't send your child to a nursery or childminder without the relevant checks, so be safe with your classes too.

Free classes Finally, re-school classes and baby groups are a fantastic way of meeting new people and making friends for both parent and child, so don't be afraid get out and about and enjoy all your local area has to offer.

Do your research, check online reviews and class feedback, and talk to the best critics of all – other parents!

Whatever play activities you decide to do with your baby - don't stress about the quality of play - all they really need is your attention and they'll be happy.

Don't feel pressured into playing super-parent with all the amazing baby sensory homemade activities about either. While following amazing baby craft pages and baby play group ideas are interesting and helpful to many, they can also make you feel a little inadequate of you don't have time to achieve what you see on social media.

Remember you also don't have to spend a fortune and you certainly don't need to sign up to every baby group and activity going. Find out what works for you - what you enjoy doing as a family, and make it a regular part of your baby's routine.

CHAPTER TWELVE: THE POORLY BABY CLUB - A LOOK INTO TEETHING AND CHILDHOOD ILLNESS

Parenting is hard even at the best of times, but when your little one gets poorly - it can be a really worrying and stressful. The vast majority of parents will experience a poorly baby in the first year. This is quite normal as your baby's immune system is busy developing. The immune system strengthens by fighting off minor illnesses, so it's all part of your little one growing.

Your baby can't tell you how they are feeling but, even without any obvious symptoms, your parental instinct will probably alert you to when your baby is not quite right.

Before we go further into this chapter and look at different illnesses, it's important to say that all babies less than three months of age with a fever should see a doctor right away.

The medical symptoms and guidance in this part of the book is taken from The National Health Service (NHS) guidance - May 2020.

Before we look into common illnesses in babyhood - it is important to note here that if your child has any of the signs listed below, you must medical help as soon as possible:

Breathing:

- Rapid breathing or panting
- A throaty noise while breathing
- Your baby is finding it hard to get their breath and is sucking their stomach in under their ribs

Other signs:

- Blue, pale, blotchy, or ashen (grey) skin
- Your baby is hard to wake up, or appears disoriented or floppy
- Your baby is crying constantly and you cannot console or distract them, or the cry does not sound like their normal cry
- Green vomit
- Your child has a *febrile seizure (fit) for the first time

- Your child is under 8 weeks old and does not want to feed
- Nappies that are drier than usual – this is a sign of dehydration

*A febrile seizure, also known as a fever fit or febrile convulsion, is a seizure associated with a high body temperature but without any serious underlying health issue. They most commonly occur in children between the ages of 6 months and 5 years.

Now we've got the scary stuff out of he way, let's take a look at common childhood illnesses, and please - if your little one is poorly it is inevitable that their sleep will be disrupted. During illness or teething - you have to just ride the knackered wave of long nights and little sleep until they are feeling better. (Don't forget the very begging of the book can help you with the Mombie/Zomdad days!)

Fever

The first sign your baby might be unwell is when they have a temperature. A normal temperature in babies and children is about 36.4C, but this can vary slightly. A high temperature or fever is usually considered to be a temperature of 38C or above.

Your baby may have a high temperature if they:

- Feel hotter than usual to touch on their forehead, back or stomach

- Feel sweaty or clammy

- Have flushed cheeks

If you think your baby has a high temperature, it's best to check their temperature with a thermometer. This can help you work out whether you need to get medical advice.

How do I take my child's temperature?

Ideally, you need a digital thermometer to get a fast, accurate reading. (You can buy these online or from pharmacies and most large supermarkets.)

To take your child's temperature:

1.   Hold them comfortably on your knee and put the thermometer in their armpit.

2.   Gently, but firmly, hold them to keep the thermometer in place for however long it says in the manufacturer's instructions – usually about 15 seconds. Some digital thermometers beep when they're ready.

3.   The display on the thermometer will then show your child's temperature.

How can I make sure the reading is accurate?

If you use a digital thermometer in your child's armpit and follow the manufacturer's instructions carefully, you should get an accurate reading.

There are a few things that can slightly alter the reading – for example, if your baby has been:

- Wrapped up tightly in a blanket

- In a very warm room or it's a hot day

- they have been very active (crawling in older babies or they have just had a big distressed crying episode)

- Wearing too many layers

- Had a bath that was too warm

If this is the case, allow them to cool down for a few minutes, but do not let them get cold or shivery, then take their temperature again to see if there's any change.

Other types of thermometer

You can buy other types of thermometer, but they may not be as accurate as a digital thermometer for taking a baby or young child's temperature:

- ear (tympanic) thermometers – these allow you to take a temperature reading from the ear and are quick but expensive; they can give misleading readings if you do not put them in the ear correctly, which can sometimes happen with babies because their ear holes are so small

- strip-type thermometers – these are held against the forehead and are not an accurate way of taking a temperature. They show the temperature of the skin, rather than the body.

You should **never** use an old-fashioned glass thermometer containing mercury. These can break, releasing small splinters of glass and highly poisonous mercury. They're no longer used in hospitals and you cannot buy them in shops.

If your child is exposed to mercury, get medical advice immediately.

What causes a high temperature in children?

A high temperature is usually a sign that your child's body is trying to fight an infection.

Some babies and young children get a high temperature after having their vaccinations. This should go away quite quickly by itself. If you're concerned, speak to a health visitor or GP.

What should I do if my baby has a high temperature?

You can usually look after your baby or child at home when they have a high temperature. Make sure you give them plenty of drinks, to avoid dehydration. If you're breastfeeding, offer your baby plenty of feeds. Take some of their layers of clothing off, and use a cool flannel on the head arms, neck and tummy to help them to feel cooler.

Always contact a GP or call 111 if:

- Your child has other signs of illness, such as a rash, as well as a high temperature

- Your baby's temperature is 38C or higher if they're under 3 months old

- Your baby's temperature is 39C or higher if they're 3 to 6 months old

If you need to speak to someone outside normal surgery hours, you can call your GP surgery's out-of-hours service (if they have one) or NHS 111.

Runny or blocked nose

A snotty, or runny nose will become a familiar sight as your baby grows. Mucus plays a big part in keeping your baby well. It lubricates and protects airways, keeping out particles and fights off invading bacteria.

Newborns can get sniffles without a cold. Normal levels of mucus build up in their tiny noses. It's hard for them to clear out mucus because they don't know how to blow through their noses. If your newborn is snuffly and it's interfering with feeding, try giving small feeds, more often, or feed a steamy bathroom. The steam is great for congestion.

As your baby gets older, a runny or blocked nose is usually a sign of the common cold.

Coughs and Colds

Coughs and colds are extremely common in little ones and tend to occur more frequently over the autumn and winter months. They are usually caused by an infection and most babies get better by themselves. In general, antibiotics do not make them better more quickly. Babies can catch several colds a year as their immune systems are more vulnerable to infections. Symptoms usually develop over a couple of days.

Symptoms: Runny or blocked nose, sneezing, sore throat, cough, headache, mild fever, tiredness, aches and pains. (some of these symptoms your baby won't be able to communicate.)

Treatment: There is no medical cure for a cold and you can only treat the symptoms and your baby will feel unsettled and want lots of cuddles and attention.

If your child has a fever, pain or discomfort, babies over 2 months, weighing over 4kg and not premature can have children's paracetamol. Always follow the dosage instructions.

Nose drops from the pharmacy or rub-on decongestant (from 3 months) may help your child breathe more easily, but check with your pharmacist or GP for advice when using these.

If your baby has a cough that has not gone away after a week, or also has a high temperature and is breathless, consult your GP, or 111(UK) for advice.

Croup

Croup is a condition that affects babies' and young children's airways. It's usually mild, but call NHS 111 or see a GP if you're worried.

Symptoms:
- a barking cough that sounds like a seal (you can search online to hear examples)
- a hoarse voice
- difficulty breathing
- a rasping sound when breathing in

Your child will usually have cold-like symptoms to begin with, such as a temperature, runny nose and cough.

Treatment: Croup symptoms usually come on after a few days and are often worse at night. A humid or moist atmosphere will ease your baby's breathing. Sit with your little one on your lap upright if you can and let them inhale the steam.

If the croup persists, call NHS 111. If your child has significant difficulty breathing, seek immediate medical help by calling 999.

Diarrhoea and vomiting

Diarrhoea and vomiting are common in adults, children and babies. They're often caused by a stomach bug and should stop in a few days. The advice is the same if you have diarrhoea and vomiting together or separately.

Treatment: You can usually treat your baby at home. The most important thing is to have lots of fluids to avoid dehydration.

- Stay at home and let your baby get plenty of rest to avoid spreading infection (diarrhoea usually stops within 5 to 7 days and vomiting usually stops in 1 or 2 days) don't let your little one go to any baby groups or childcare for 48 hours after the loose stool or vomit episode to avoid spreading infection.

- Carry on breast or bottle feeding your baby – if they're being sick, try giving small feeds, more often than usual.

- Give babies on formula or solid foods small sips of water between feeds

- If your baby has been weaned - let them eat if they feel able to but don't force them.

- Wash any soiled clothing or bedding separately on a hot wash right away.

- Wash hands regularly when dealing with your baby to avoid catching D&V yourself.

Chicken Pox

Chickenpox is a common childhood illness caused by the caused by the varicella zoster virus, that most children will catch at some point in their lives.

The virus is caught from spreading through the air and through direct contact with fluid from the blisters on skin that the virus causes. It's more common under the age of ten years old, so it's likely your little one will experience this illness during the nursery and primary school years.

Chicken pox is extremely common as it is highly infectious; being spread by coughing, sneezing or by directly touching the rash.

Many parents are now considering purchasing the recently available two-course vaccine to spare their little ones suffering the ill-effects of Chickenpox.

There are two chickenpox vaccines currently available to children **12 months and over.**

Symptoms:

- loss of appetite.
- A mild flu like illness is usually present before the appearance of the rash.
- A red, itchy rash which blisters.

Treatment: Although there's no specific medical treatment there are things you can do to help your baby.

• Pain relief such as children's paracetamol (if your baby is over 2 months old) can help if your child has pain or a fever. Do not use infant ibuprofen or nuprofen.

• Antihistamines or calamine lotion may help with the itching - but check with GP/Pharmacist before giving/using on your baby.

• Change and wash bed linen, nightwear and clothing regularly.

• Keep fingernails short to avoid scratching the skin

• Babies with Chickenpox should stay at home until the blisters have crusted over and avoid contact with pregnant women.

• Chicken pox is usually mild but once in a while complications can occur. If you have concerns at any time call NHS 111.

Meningitis

Meningitis means swelling of the lining around the brain and spinal cord. It can be hard to recognise at first.

Symptoms: Symptoms of meningitis can appear in any order. Some may not appear at all. In the early stages, there may not be a rash, or the rash may fade on pressure. **You should get medical help immediately if you're concerned about yourself or your child. Trust your instincts and do not wait until a rash develops.**

Symptoms of meningitis, septicaemia and meningococcal disease include:

- A high temperature
- Cold hands and feet
- Vomiting
- Confusion
- Breathing quickly
- Muscle and joint pain
- pale, mottled or blotchy skin
- Spots or a rash

- Headache
- A stiff neck
- A dislike of bright lights
- Being very sleepy or difficult to wake
- Fits (seizures)

Babies may also:

- Refuse feeds
- Be irritable
- Have a high-pitched cry
- Have a stiff body or be floppy or unresponsive
- Have a bulging soft spot on the top of their head

Someone with meningitis, septicaemia or meningococcal disease can get a lot worse very quickly.

Call 999 for an ambulance or go to your nearest A&E if you think you or your baby might be seriously ill.

Sticky eyes and conjunctivitis

Sticky eyes are common in newborn babies and young children while their tear ducts are developing. If you notice this and it continues for more than 24 hours, contact your health visitor or GP.

Conjunctivitis can be passed on easily, so wash your hands and use a separate towel for your baby.

Symptoms: You may see some sticky stuff in the corner of the eyes or their eyelashes may be stuck together.

Treatment: It normally clears up on its own, but you may have to clean your baby's eyes regularly with damp cotton wool.

- Use clean, cooled boiled water to do this.

- Wipe each eye from the corner by the nose outwards. Use a clean piece of cotton wool for each wipe.

- Remember to wash your hands before and afterwards and avoid sharing towels to prevent spreading infection.

Rashes

It's normal for babies to develop rashes early on as their skin adapts to a different environment. If your baby develops a rash and seems unwell contact your GP.

Most rashes are nothing to worry about but do be aware of the signs of meningitis. Go to A&E or call 999 if your child has a rash and they:

- Have a stiff neck
- Are bothered by light
- Seem confused
- Are shaking uncontrollably
- Have a fever you can't control
- Have unusually cold hands and feet
- Have a rash that doesn't fade when you press a glass against it

These can be signs of meningitis.
Other rashes include:

Nappy rash

Nappy rash is very common and can affect lots of babies. It is usually caused when your baby's skin comes into contact with wee and poo that collects in their nappy. A nappy rash causes your baby's skin to become sore.

Most nappy rashes can be treated with a simple skincare routine and by using a cream you can get from the pharmacist. With a mild nappy rash, your baby won't normally feel too much discomfort.

Dry skin

A baby's skin is thinner and needs extra care. Dry, flaky skin, some blemishes, blotches and slight rashes are normal in newborns and will naturally clear up. If your baby is otherwise well but has a rash and you are worried about it contact your health visitor.

Heat rash

Heat rash is uncomfortable, but usually harmless. It should clear up on its own after a few days.

Symptoms

- Small red spots
- An itchy, prickly feeling
- Redness and mild swelling

It can appear anywhere on the body and spread, but it's not infectious to other people. The main thing to do is keep your baby's skin cool in hot weather so they are less likely to develop a rash.

Treatment

- Wear loose cotton clothing
- Use lightweight bedding
- Use a cool damp washcloth or cotton wool to soothe skin.
- Drink plenty of fluid to avoid dehydration

To calm the itching or prickly rash:

- Apply something cold, such as a damp cloth or ice pack (wrapped in a tea towel) for no more than 20 minutes

- Tap or pat the rash instead of scratching it

- Do not use perfumed shower gels or creams on your baby

Speak to a pharmacist about heat rash. They can give advice and suggest the best treatment to use.

A pharmacist might recommend:

- Calamine lotion

- Antihistamine tablets

- Hydrocortisone cream (though not really suitable for little ones under 10 or pregnant so seek advice from a doctor before using this treatment.)

Hives

Hives rashes usually settle down within a few minutes to a few days. You can often treat hives yourself.

Hives can be different sizes and shapes, and appear anywhere on the body. The rash is often itchy and sometimes feels like it's stinging or burning so your baby will be unsettled.

If you aren't sure it's Hives. Your GP can give you advice about the rash and treatment to bring down your baby's hives rash.

Call 999 right away if your baby's hives are accompanied by serious symptoms like trouble breathing or swallowing, mouth or lip swelling, or nausea or vomiting. These can all be signs of anaphylaxis, which is life-threatening.

Slapped cheek syndrome

Slapped cheek syndrome (fifth disease) is common in children and should clear up on its own within 3 weeks. It's rarer in adults, but can be more serious.

The first sign of slapped cheek syndrome is usually feeling unwell for a few days.

Symptoms

- A high temperature of 38C or more

- A runny nose and sore throat

- A headache

- A bright red rash may appear on both cheeks. It may look as if your baby's cheeks have been slapped.

- A few days later, a lighter-coloured rash may appear on the chest, arms and legs. The skin is raised and can be itchy.

You do not usually need to see a GP for slapped cheek syndrome, but there are some things you can do to ease symptoms.

Treatment

- Babies should continue their normal feeds

- Take paracetamol or ibuprofen for a high temperature, headaches or joint pain

- Use moisturiser on itchy skin (Ask your local Pharmacist for advice)

- Speak to a pharmacist if your baby has itchy skin – they can recommend the best antihistamine for children.

If you have any concerns or your baby develops any other symptoms - contact your GP for medical advice.

Hand, foot and mouth disease

Hand, foot and mouth disease is a common childhood illness that can affect adults. It usually clears up by itself in 7 to 10 days.

Symptoms

The first signs of hand, foot and mouth disease can be:

- A sore throat
- A high temperature, above 38C
- Not wanting to eat/feed

After a few days mouth ulcers and a rash will appear.

You cannot take antibiotics or medicines to cure hand, foot and mouth disease. It has to run its course. It usually gets better in 7 to 10 days.

Treatment

• Drink fluids to prevent dehydration – avoid acidic drinks, such as fruit juice

- If your baby has weaned already - give soft foods like soup and avoid hot or spicy foods

- Take paracetamol or ibuprofen to help ease a sore mouth or throat (always check dosage amount for age)

Speak to a pharmacist for advice about treatments, such as mouth ulcer gels, sprays and mouthwashes, to relieve pain. They can tell you which ones are suitable for babies.

Scarlet fever

Scarlet fever is a contagious infection that mostly affects young children. It's easily treated with antibiotics.

Symptoms

The first signs of scarlet fever can be flu-like symptoms, including a high temperature of 38C or above, a sore throat and swollen neck glands (a large lump on the side of your neck).

A rash appears a few days later. The rash feels like sandpaper and starts on the chest and tummy. On lighter skin it looks pink or red. On darker skin it can be more difficult to see, but you can still feel it.

A white coating also appears on the tongue. This peels, leaving it red and swollen.

Treatment

See a GP if your baby:

- Has scarlet fever symptoms
- Does not get better in a week (after seeing a GP), especially if your child has recently had chickenpox
- Is ill again weeks after scarlet fever has cleared up – this can be a sign of a complication, such as rheumatic fever
- Is feeling unwell and have been in contact with someone who has scarlet fever

Scarlet fever is very infectious. Check with a GP before you go in. They may suggest a phone consultation.

Measles

Measles can be prevented by having the measles, mumps and rubella (MMR) vaccine. This is given in 2 doses as part of the NHS childhood vaccination programme.

Measles starts with cold-like symptoms that develop about 10 days after becoming infected. This is followed a few days later by the measles rash.

For most people, the illness lasts around 7 to 10 days.

Symptoms

- A runny or blocked nose
- Sneezing
- Watery eyes
- Swollen eyelids
- Sore, red eyes that may be sensitive to light
- A high temperature (fever), which may reach around 40C (104F)
- Small greyish-white spots in the mouth
- Aches and pains
- A cough
- Loss of appetite
- Tiredness, irritability, and a general lack of energy

Not everyone with measles has these spots, but if someone has them in addition to the other symptoms listed above or a rash, it's highly likely they have the condition. The spots will usually last for a few days.

The measles rash appears around 2 to 4 days after the initial symptoms and normally fades after about a week. Your baby will usually feel most ill on the first or second day after the rash develops.

The rash:

- is made up of small red-brown, flat, or slightly raised spots that may join together into larger blotchy patches

- usually first appears on the head or neck before spreading outwards to the rest of the body

- is slightly itchy for some people

- can look similar to other childhood conditions, such as slapped cheek syndrome, roseola or rubella

- is unlikely to be caused by measles if the person has been fully vaccinated (had 2 doses of the MMR vaccine) or had measles before.

Treatment

Contact a GP as soon as possible if you suspect that you or your child has measles, even if you're not completely sure.

It's best to phone before your visit, as the GP surgery may need to make arrangements to reduce the risk of spreading the infection to others. You should also see a GP if you have been in close contact with someone who has measles and have not been fully vaccinated or haven't had the infection before, even if you do not have any symptoms yet.

Measles is a highly infectious viral illness that can be very unpleasant and sometimes lead to serious complications. It's now uncommon in the UK because of the effectiveness of vaccination.

There are several things you can do to help relieve your symptoms and reduce the risk of spreading the infection.
These include:

- taking paracetamol or ibuprofen to relieve fever, aches and pains (aspirin should not be given to children under 16 years old)

- drinking plenty of water to avoid dehydration

- closing the curtains to help reduce light sensitivity

- using damp cotton wool to clean the eyes

- staying off school or work for at least 4 days from when the rash first appears

In severe cases, especially if there are complications, you or your child may need to be admitted to hospital for treatment.

Impetigo

Impetigo is a skin infection that's very contagious but not usually serious. It often gets better in 7 to 10 days if you get treatment. Anyone can get it, but it's very common in young children.

Impetigo starts with red sores or blisters. They quickly burst and leave crusty, golden-brown patches.

These can:

- look a bit like cornflakes stuck to your baby's skin
- get bigger

- spread to other parts of your baby's body

- be itchy

- sometimes be painful

See your GP if:

- You think your baby might have impetigo

- Your baby had treatment for impetigo but the symptoms change or get worse

- Your baby had impetigo before and it keeps coming back

Impetigo is very infectious. Check with the GP before you go in to the practice. They may suggest a phone consultation.

Your baby is likely to suffer from quite a few sniffles, rashes and tummy upsets over the next few years. Their little immune system is still maturing, and so, they are more prone to minor illnesses than older children.

Whatever mild illness your 'poorly baby club' member is suffering from, the best way to soothe your baby is to give them lots of love and attention and to just ride the poorly way until they feel much better.

If at any time you have any concerns - seek medical advice right away. Trust your instincts always and don't worry that you are overthinking or overreacting. Remember - you know your baby best.

CHAPTER THIRTEEN: THE WIDE AWAKE TODDLER CLUB - A LOOK INTO THINGS TO COME.

The first 12 months can fly by in a flash and you'll suddenly find yourself with a walking, chattery toddler.

No sooner have you sorted your baby's sleep and had a nice long spell of happy bedtimes and decent sleep, when your toddler starts suddenly waking in the night.

The toddler years are often challenging, but even more so when your peaceful, happy-sleeping little one turns into a wakeful toddler. This is called *toddler sleep regression* and these nightmare-nights can suddenly come out of the blue and leave both parents and toddlers feeling exhausted.

There are so many reasons why your super-sleeper may suddenly turn into a night-owl, but try not to worry, for whatever reason your toddler is waking, be reassured that this won't last for too long. With lots of patience and by being consistent in your methods, this little blip in the sleep routine will soon be far behind you.

In my next book 'The Wide Awake toddler Club' we will take a look into all of the reasons why your toddler might be waking in the night.

Chapters include:

Chapter One: Why is sleep important, and how much does my toddler need?

Chapter Two: The Midnight Toddler - What to do when your child refuses to go to bed (or wakes up in the night and hops in with you!)

Chapter Three: The 'I'm not tired' brigade - What to do when your toddler struggles to fall asleep!

Chapter Four: Things that go bump in the night: How to deal with night fears, nightmares and night terrors.

Chapter Five: Ch,ch,changes - Getting back into good sleep habits after childcare holidays and clock changes!

Chapter Six: Anxiety and the sleep deprived: Tips for calming and coping with an anxious toddler.

Chapter Seven: Jump around! Jump around! Jump up jump up and.. (Get some sleep!) How physical activity with your toddler creates better sleep!

Chapter Eight: The Hippy Toddler Club - How Kids Yoga and Mindful Meditation can aid sleep.

Chapter Nine: Toddler Bedrooms - How comfortable surroundings make better sleep spaces.

Chapter Ten: The Noisy Sleeper - A look into Childhood Snoring and Sleep Apnoea

Chapter Eleven: The Wide Awake Kids Club - A look into things to come in the primary school years.

CHAPTER FOURTEEN: THE WIDE AWAKE BABY CLUB ENDORSEMENTS.

I've been fortunate enough to work with many wonderful families, high profile parents, celebrities and professionals over the years, and thought it might be beneficial (so you can see if this stuff in my book actually works,) to ask them to share their experiences of my advice.

I paid them all a squillion quid each obviously, to say ace things about me, meaning even if you bought this cheap-as chips guide, I'll be forever paying off these people with the profits. Don't feel bad for me though. Just pop a nice review on Amazon and it'll be a bestseller in no time, and I'll soon be debt free from these scoundrels.

Here's what a few of them had to say...

'I've known Fi personally and professionally for many years. She's widely respected within the childcare and early years field, known for her professionalism, trusted in her area of expertise and, most of all, her approachable nature. BAPN members are aware of her amazing work and tell us how they use her website 'Childcare is Fun!' as their recommended 'go to guide' for the parents they work for, in particular new and sometimes anxious mums and dads.

I'm thrilled to be endorsing Fi's latest book and just know everyone who reads it will feel they know Fi and will benefit hugely from all they'll take from within it.'

- **Tricia Pritchard, MD BAPN (The Professional Association for Professional Nannies)**

'Fi Star-Stone is a regular contributor for Mother & Baby magazine, giving her invaluable and expert advice on all things sleep, toddlers and parenting. Her sleep tips are a must-read for any parent!'

- **Aimee Jakes, Digital Editor, Mother & Baby**

'Good sleep is just as important for older children as it is for babies and this is a clear, practical guide, to ensuring your child gets all the sleep they need. There is something to suit all parenting styles to lead the way to a good night's sleep for the whole family.'

- **Nicola Watson, Child Sleep Consultant, BA (Hons)**

'Fi has been the ear I've needed when I've doubted everything I thought I knew about being a parent. She doesn't judge and speaks (honestly) from her own experiences as a mother'

- **Kate, Mum of one from same-sex blog 'Lesbemums'**

'Fi's advice saved my sanity and my marriage!

We thought we'd had a tough time with our first baby who wasn't keen on sleep for the first 6 months, but when baby number two was still waking 2 hourly at 9 months old and would not nap we were at breaking point.

Well-meaning advice from Health Care Professionals left me sitting on the stairs sobbing each night while by baby screamed herself sick.

Fi's gentle, practical and realistic advice and support meant that we weren't having hours of screaming and as a couple we were able to get on the same side and work together.

We worked with our youngest to find a pattern which worked for her and us and over two weeks we went from 6 or 7 wakings in the night to 2!

Fi's book is always on our new parent gifts list. I cannot recommend her highly enough.'

- **Charlotte Goodyear - Mum of two**

'Fi has been so great offering advice to me at several stages in the last few years. She provides ongoing support, really takes on board any problems and offers relevant and helpful advice which has helped us out so much.
She has a wealth of knowledge on sleep issues and this has been invaluable at times when I did not know where to turn.

- **Lisa Hodson, Mum of Two**

'Fi has an extensive knowledge and experience of childcare spanning over many years, and now with her own two children. Her kindness comes through in the way she offers advice and help without judgment or preaching.

Fi's books are the perfect 'go to' for all parents. I adore Fi and her gentle approach to parenting.'

- Kelly Shrehorn -Mum of Five.

'Knowing Fi is like having a parenting guardian angel around in your time of need or even just for a lighthearted parenting chuckle. My motherhood goddess with so much zest for life & supporting others that is comfort blanket we all need at the end of the day to tell you, mama you've got this.'

- Rosie B, Juggling Mum of three under 4

'Fi has a wealth of knowledge, and her non-judgmental attitude means you can literally ask her anything! This comes across in her books and they are great for advice when it comes to a troublesome toddler or even just a bit of reassurance everything will be OK!'

- Ceri Watt Mum of Two

'A modern, individual, realistic parenting guru!'

- Steve Camsell, Uncle of Three

'Fi's practical advice and guidance was a much needed support to us when our son wouldn't sleep. Her sleep tips helped us enormously!'

- Emma Shilton, Mum of Two, blogger at 'Life According to Mrs Shilts'

'Fi is a true inspiration in so many ways. The most incredible mum! Her zest for life and positivity just shines through everything she does.

I love the way she makes anything seem possible even in tough times - makes me realise that we can make our dreams happen with the right attitude.

A heart of gold and a love for helping people and being the best mum and version of herself at all times. What is there not to love!

Thank you Fi, for all your positivity and for being you! You rock!'

- **Laura Chelmick, Professional Nanny, (Professional Nanny of The Year 2005) Maternity Nurse and Mum of one**

'I have had the pleasure of knowing Fi for many years now and she has been an invaluable help with all 3 of my children over my 10 year parenting journey.

Both my boys have sleep apnea, so sleep has always been quite an issue for us in our household but in particular Fi has been my middle of the night support when I felt I was at a loss.

Our eldest son is severely disabled and does not produce Melatonin, Fi time after time has researched to find ways to help Grayson and I to find ways to help him sleep when his body tells him not to.

She is our real life Mary Poppins at the end of a message and her first books have been picked up by us many many times.'

- **Kara Spencer - Mum of Three**

CHAPTER FIFTEEN: NIGHT-NIGHT FROM FI!

Are you sitting comfortably? Then I'll begin...

So many parents ask me if I 'practice what I preach' and honestly? Yes I do - but not just for my little ones and their wellbeing - it's for my wellbeing too! It's about quality time and 'switch-off' time from being a mum! (It's also about having a good old Netflixathon, dinner and a cheeky Vimto in peace - we really need that time as parents!)

My two are currently (as I write this,) 9 and 10 years old, and have honestly been in a great daily and bedtime routine since they were 6 weeks old.

Of course we've fallen out of the routine many times with holidays and school summer breaks, and there's always a few weekend late nights here and there. These late nights however, are few and far between as I have learned valuable lessons from experience. Any regular break in the routine usually has consequences! They are always shattered and very grumpy the next morning. It was the same when they were babies.

I've come to realise that even though mine aren't babies anymore - they still really need their sleep, and their routine and it's why I always insist on the early bedtime on school nights.

In all honesty - sometimes we have had, and still sometimes have, times when bedtime isn't a nice time. The bad moods, over tiredness, arguments or messing about or the poorly nights can make it a pretty stressful time, but the majority of nights, nine times out of ten, they have always gone to bed happily and content and slept really well.

People say I'm lucky I have good sleepers, but I honestly don't think it's about luck. It's about routine, consistency and hard work in the early years, it's also about not slipping into bad routines which can be so easily done - especially in the summer when the weather is nice and you lose track of time in the garden.

The thing I always say to parents is there is no right or wrong way to approach sleep as a parent. You do what works for you and your family.

If love to co-sleep (safely) with your 6 month, if you love your 9 month old staying up with you until 9.30pm every night, if you don't mind your 10 month old waking you every night at 3am - then it is nobody's business but yours. If you are all happy and getting good sleep then why should it matter?

What I'm saying is, you should always make an informed choice when it comes to your child's sleep; please just do makes you happy or gets you and your child the most sleep at the time. Maybe you are having a few problems but don't feel ready to tackle them just yet - that's cool. This book is ready to pick up and put down anytime.

If your baby's sleeping problems haven't been resolved by trying my gentle techniques and guidance in this book, and you have real concerns for certain sleep behaviours or are worried there is something troublesome about their sleeping patterns, or you are struggling to cope, then it is important to seek extra help from your GP or qualified sleep professional.

Please remember there is absolutely nothing to feel ashamed of, or be embarrassed by, when it comes to asking for help as a parent. Sleep is an incredibly difficult thing to master and nobody will judge you for seeking extra help.

There are lots of trained sleep professionals online who offer private sleep packages to help you with your child's sleep issues, some of my absolute faves, who I've had the privilege of working with over the years, I've shared at the back of this book. My advice online is for FREE, and always has been, but it is only via message or email and I don't offer phonically or home visits. This is why I don't charge.

Please be aware, that there are many *parenting experts*' and '*sleep experts*' out there that have no qualifications, training or experience, so please do check references, qualifications, recommendations and choose wisely before booking a consultation.

I'm always around on social media if you just need a reassuring *'hey - you got this! Trust your instincts!'* message from me.

Finally, thank you so much for buying this little baby sleep guide of mine. I really hope you've enjoyed it and it has offered reassurance, guidance and a little humour. But above all - I hope it brings you the gift of happy sleep.

Much love, Fi xx

CHAPTER SIXTEEN: THE WIDE AWAKE BABY CLUB CREW - BOOK REFERENCES, AWESOME PRIVATE SLEEP CONSULTANTS AND COOL PARENTING BLOGGERS TO FOLLOW.

Book References:

- **Safe Sleeping guidance:** Lullaby Trust www.lullabytrust.org.uk

- **Swaddling:**

  - Quote from Rachel Moon, MD, FAAP. - www.healthychildren.org

  - The British philosopher John Locke (1632–1704) 1693 publication *Some Thoughts Concerning Education*

  - *Felix Würtz (approx 1500-1598)*

- **Childhood/baby common illnesses:**

  - National Health Service - www.NHS.co.uk

- **Sleep research:**

  - The American Academy of Pediatrics (AAP)

  - National Institute of Neurological Disorders and Stroke (NINDS)

  - Han-Seok Seo - The Effects of Coffee Bean Aroma on the Rat Brain Stressed by Sleep Deprivation

- **Childhood illness**

  -National Health Service (NHS)

Child Sleep Consultants recommended by Fi:

NicolaWatson - www.childsleepsolutions.co.uk

During her diverse career, Nicola has helped countless children, their parents and carers to get a better night's sleep. She has a BA (Hons) in Social Science and Psychology and is an OCN accredited Child Sleep Consultant.

Nicola is a member of the professional body the British Sleep Society and the Sleep Professionals Association as well as the Child Psychology Group. Nicola has written articles on sleep for the NCT and has trained both parents and professionals on teaching babies and children to sleep through the night.

But perhaps most significantly Nicola is herself a mother who really understands the importance of a good night's sleep to families and most importantly to the child. Nicola is based in Chislehurst, South East London/Kent.

- **JoTantum** - www.JoTantum.com

With 30 years experience working with babies and parents worldwide, Jo is passionate about teaching babies how to love sleeping, with calm, gentle, guidance - all with no tears!

Jo's bestselling book *Baby Secrets* has helped families around the world and she also offers email, phone and Skype support. Jo's *Sleep Angel's* are a team of gentle sleep trainers, and offer overnight 'Rescue Packages' via her website.

You have probably seen Jo at one of The Baby Shows around the country, as one of their key speakers or on Daybreak as their Baby Expert. Jo has also appeared on ITN news, BBC Radio, and in many popular parenting magazines.

Most importantly, Jo is a mother herself, so understands the importance of sleep for all the family.

Jo is based in The Midlands, in the UK.

Parenting sites and bloggers to follow

- **Childcare is Fun** Fi's main website - www.childcareisfun.co.uk

- **The Regular Parent** Fi's podcast site - www.theregularparent.co.uk

- **BAPN** - Professional Nanny Organisation www.bapn.org.uk

- **Mother&BabyMagazine** - www.motherandbaby.co.uk

- **Lesbemums** - Parenting Blog - www.lesbemums.com

- **Hollybobs** - Parenting Blog - www.hollybobbs.co.uk

- **kellysvintagemakes** - Parenting blog and homemade jewellery

  kellysvintagemakes.blogspot.com

- **Kara Spencer** -Parenting and lifestyle blog - www.innocentcharmchats.co.uk

- **Life According to Mrs Shilts** - Parenting Blog www.mrsshilts.co.uk

- **Molly Forbes** - Body confidence presenter and Blogger - www.mothersawlaysright.com

- **Laura Chelmick** - *For you and your Baby'* Professional parenting service - www.foryouandyourbaby.com

Family Lives: An organisation providing immediate help from volunteer parent support workers 24 hours a day, 7 days a week.
- helpline: 0808 800 2222
- website: www.familylives.org.uk

Family Rights Group: Support for parents and other family members whose children are involved with or need social care services.
- helpline: 0808 801 0366
- website: www.frg.org.uk

Gingerbread: single parents, equal families
Help and advice on the issues that matter to lone parents.
- helpline: 0808 802 0925
- website: www.gingerbread.org.uk

Pink Parents: Pink Parents offer a range of support services and social activities for all Lesbian, Gay, Bisexual and Transsexual families, whether you are considering parenting, have grandchildren, are fostering or adopting or are an Uncle or Aunty, PinkParents can offer you support and a place to meet new friends.
- website: pinkparents.org.uk

PANDAS foundation: Pre and Post Natal Depression Advice and Support.

- helpline: 0808 1961 776. Open 9am - 8pm - 7 days a week.
- website: www.pandasfoundation.org.uk

MIND: postnatal depression and other perinatal mental health problems
Website: www.mind.org
infoline: 0300 123 3393
Email: info@mind.org.uk
Text: 86463

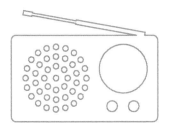

THE REGULAR PARENT PODCAST

The Regular Parent Podcast is available now on iTunes!

"I was overwhelmed by the amount of messages and emails I had received over the past few months from worried parents who felt their lives were not 'normal.'

So many feel they are 'not enough' when scrolling through 'instagram perfect' pics, so I decided to start this little project to show them (and the listener,) that every family is different, every child is different, and every parent is different.

That a regular parent – is a parent like you and like me, your life is 'your kind of normal,' and you shouldn't compare it to others. I'm delighted that so many lovely parents have wanted to be involved and I can't wait to share with you this wonderful series of podcasts.

'The Regular Parent' series, takes a look at parenting from the eyes of *regular parents* like you and me. Weekly podcast interviews with real 'everyday' parents and the everyday amazing things they do. So grab yourself a cuppa (or a glass of something nice,) curl up on the sofa and listen to our lovely, regular families share their lives.

From single parents holding down full time jobs and juggling it all, to parents who have little ones with disabilities – 'The Regular Parent' aims to bring all parents together in this new podcast series looking at the lives of regular parents, like you, and like me from all around the world.

The Regular Parent Podcast is available to listen to on iTunes and via the Regular Parent website www.TheRegularParent.co.uk"

ABOUT THE AUTHOR

As a mum of two little ones born less than a year apart, Fi Star-Stone knows that parenting isn't always easy. Her gentle techniques and approachable manner are popular with families and celebrities worldwide and many parents refer to her as *'the nice expert!'*

Fi is a qualified parenting advisor with over 27 years working with children and families. Her qualifications include a Degree in Childhood and Youth studies, an NNEB in Nursery Nursing, and a Diploma in Childhood studies.

Her bestselling books *'The Baby Bedtime Book - Say goodnight to Sleepless Nights'* and *'The Wide Awake kids Club'* have been helping parents to give their little ones the gift of happy sleep worldwide!

Fi's bestselling lockdown journal for children *'My Thinky Thoughts'* has helped hundreds of families to get their children talking about their feelings during the 2020 Global Covid-19 Pandemic.

In 2005 and 2006 Fi was 'highly commended' by The Professional Association of Nursery Nurses for her work with children in her role as a professional Nanny.

Fi writes for parenting magazines and websites and is often on BBC radio talking all things parenting, she's also joined the fire-service as an on-call fire-fighter but had to sadly resign in 2020 due to injury.

Likes: Moomins, Cake and kitchen dancing.
Dislikes: Very early mornings and unkind people.
Favourite Music: The Killers, Pink, and David Bowie.

Follow Fi:

Twitter @FiStarStone
Instagram @FiStarStone
Facebook Childcare is Fun!
YouTube: Fi Star-Stone
Podcast: 'The Regular Parent' available on iTunes #TheRegularParent
Press enquiries: Fi@Childcareisfun.co.uk

ABOUT THE ILLUSTRATOR

As an aspiring professional illustrator, Orla is heading to Staffordshire University in Autumn 2020 to study for a BA honours in illustration.

Orla started her business *'Orla-Hope Art'* at the age of sixteen and sells a range of products from prints to t-shirts. Her aim is to spread positivity within her work, by using bright colour and inspirational quotes that she hopes brighten a person's day to day life. Orla takes inspiration from her favourite things such a yoga, mindfulness and houseplants.

Likes: Houseplants, her Cavapoo Mabel, herbal tea and lots of napping.

Dislikes: Coffee, Icy weather and rude people

Favourite Music: Harry Styles, The Beatles and Fleetwood Mac

Follow Orla:

Instagram @orlahopeart

Facebook Orla Hope Art

Illustration enquiries: orlahopeart@gmail.com

THE WIDE AWAKE KIDS CLUB - SIMPLE SOLUTIONS FOR KNACKERED PARENTS

Copyright © 2020 Fi Star-Stone

The information provided in this book is designed to provide helpful information on the subjects discussed. This book is not meant to be used, nor should it be used, to diagnose or treat any medical condition. For diagnosis or treatment of any medical problem, consult your own medical professional. The publisher and author are not responsible for any specific health or allergy needs that may require medical supervision and are not liable for any damages or negative consequences from any treatment, action, application or preparation, to any person reading or following the information in this book. References are provided for informational purposes only and do not constitute endorsement of any websites or other sources. Readers should be aware that the websites listed in this book may change.

MY BABY'S ROUTINE

FEEDING:

Time _____ am/pm _____ amount taken

Time _____ am/pm _____ amount taken

Time _____ am/pm _____ amount taken

Time _____ am/pm _____ amount taken

Time _____ am/pm _____ amount taken

Time _____ am/pm _____ amount taken

NAPS:

Time _____ am/pm Length of nap ……. Minutes

Time _____ am/pm Length of nap ……. Minutes

Time _____ am/pm Length of nap ……. Minutes

Time _____ am/pm Length of nap ……. Minutes

NOTES _____

_____

NOTES

MY BABY'S ROUTINE

FEEDING:

Time _____ am/pm _____ amount taken

Time _____ am/pm _____ amount taken

Time _____ am/pm _____ amount taken

Time _____ am/pm _____ amount taken

Time _____ am/pm _____ amount taken

Time _____ am/pm _____ amount taken

NAPS:

Time _____ am/pm Length of nap .... Minutes

Time _____ am/pm Length of nap .... Minutes

Time _____ am/pm Length of nap .... Minutes

Time _____ am/pm Length of nap .... Minutes

NOTES _____

_____

NOTES

MY BABY'S ROUTINE

FEEDING:

Time _____ am/pm _____ amount taken

Time _____ am/pm _____ amount taken

Time _____ am/pm _____ amount taken

Time _____ am/pm _____ amount taken

Time _____ am/pm _____ amount taken

Time _____ am/pm _____ amount taken

NAPS:

Time _____ am/pm Length of nap .... Minutes

Time _____ am/pm Length of nap .... Minutes

Time _____ am/pm Length of nap .... Minutes

Time _____ am/pm Length of nap .... Minutes

NOTES _____

_____

NOTES

_____

_____

_____

_____

_____

_____

_____

_____

_____

_____

_____

_____

_____

MY BABY'S ROUTINE

FEEDING:

Time _____ am/pm _____ amount taken

Time _____ am/pm _____ amount taken

Time _____ am/pm _____ amount taken

Time _____ am/pm _____ amount taken

Time _____ am/pm _____ amount taken

Time _____ am/pm _____ amount taken

NAPS:

Time _____ am/pm Length of nap .... Minutes

Time _____ am/pm Length of nap .... Minutes

Time _____ am/pm Length of nap .... Minutes

Time _____ am/pm Length of nap .... Minutes

NOTES _____

_____

NOTES

MY BABY'S ROUTINE

FEEDING:

Time _____ am/pm _____ amount taken

Time _____ am/pm _____ amount taken

Time _____ am/pm _____ amount taken

Time _____ am/pm _____ amount taken

Time _____ am/pm _____ amount taken

Time _____ am/pm _____ amount taken

NAPS:

Time _____ am/pm Length of nap .... Minutes

Time _____ am/pm Length of nap .... Minutes

Time _____ am/pm Length of nap .... Minutes

Time _____ am/pm Length of nap .... Minutes

NOTES _____

_____

NOTES

MY BABY'S ROUTINE

FEEDING:

Time _____ am/pm _____ amount taken

Time _____ am/pm _____ amount taken

Time _____ am/pm _____ amount taken

Time _____ am/pm _____ amount taken

Time _____ am/pm _____ amount taken

Time _____ am/pm _____ amount taken

NAPS:

Time _____ am/pm Length of nap .... Minutes

Time _____ am/pm Length of nap .... Minutes

Time _____ am/pm Length of nap .... Minutes

Time _____ am/pm Length of nap .... Minutes

NOTES _____

_____

NOTES

MY BABY'S ROUTINE

FEEDING:

Time _____ am/pm _____ amount taken

Time _____ am/pm _____ amount taken

Time _____ am/pm _____ amount taken

Time _____ am/pm _____ amount taken

Time _____ am/pm _____ amount taken

Time _____ am/pm _____ amount taken

NAPS:

Time _____ am/pm Length of nap ……. Minutes

Time _____ am/pm Length of nap ……. Minutes

Time _____ am/pm Length of nap ……. Minutes

Time _____ am/pm Length of nap ……. Minutes

NOTES _____

_____

NOTES

MY BABY'S ROUTINE

FEEDING:

Time _____ am/pm _____ amount taken

Time _____ am/pm _____ amount taken

Time _____ am/pm _____ amount taken

Time _____ am/pm _____ amount taken

Time _____ am/pm _____ amount taken

Time _____ am/pm _____ amount taken

NAPS:

Time _____ am/pm Length of nap .... Minutes

Time _____ am/pm Length of nap .... Minutes

Time _____ am/pm Length of nap .... Minutes

Time _____ am/pm Length of nap .... Minutes

NOTES _____

_____

NOTES

_____

_____

_____

_____

_____

_____

_____

_____

_____

_____

_____

_____

MY BABY'S ROUTINE

FEEDING:

Time _____ am/pm _____ amount taken

Time _____ am/pm _____ amount taken

Time _____ am/pm _____ amount taken

Time _____ am/pm _____ amount taken

Time _____ am/pm _____ amount taken

Time _____ am/pm _____ amount taken

NAPS:

Time _____ am/pm Length of nap .... Minutes

Time _____ am/pm Length of nap .... Minutes

Time _____ am/pm Length of nap .... Minutes

Time _____ am/pm Length of nap .... Minutes

NOTES _____

_____

NOTES

_____

_____

_____

_____

_____

_____

_____

_____

_____

_____

_____

_____

_____

MY BABY'S ROUTINE

FEEDING:

Time _____ am/pm _____ amount taken

Time _____ am/pm _____ amount taken

Time _____ am/pm _____ amount taken

Time _____ am/pm _____ amount taken

Time _____ am/pm _____ amount taken

Time _____ am/pm _____ amount taken

NAPS:

Time _____ am/pm Length of nap .... Minutes

Time _____ am/pm Length of nap .... Minutes

Time _____ am/pm Length of nap .... Minutes

Time _____ am/pm Length of nap .... Minutes

NOTES _____

_____

NOTES

MY BABY'S ROUTINE

FEEDING:

Time _____ am/pm _____ amount taken

Time _____ am/pm _____ amount taken

Time _____ am/pm _____ amount taken

Time _____ am/pm _____ amount taken

Time _____ am/pm _____ amount taken

Time _____ am/pm _____ amount taken

NAPS:

Time _____ am/pm Length of nap .... Minutes

Time _____ am/pm Length of nap .... Minutes

Time _____ am/pm Length of nap .... Minutes

Time _____ am/pm Length of nap .... Minutes

NOTES _____

_____

NOTES

MY BABY'S ROUTINE

FEEDING:

Time _____ am/pm _____ amount taken

Time _____ am/pm _____ amount taken

Time _____ am/pm _____ amount taken

Time _____ am/pm _____ amount taken

Time _____ am/pm _____ amount taken

Time _____ am/pm _____ amount taken

NAPS:

Time _____ am/pm Length of nap .... Minutes

Time _____ am/pm Length of nap .... Minutes

Time _____ am/pm Length of nap .... Minutes

Time _____ am/pm Length of nap .... Minutes

NOTES _____

_____

NOTES

MY BABY'S ROUTINE

FEEDING:

Time _____ am/pm _____ amount taken

Time _____ am/pm _____ amount taken

Time _____ am/pm _____ amount taken

Time _____ am/pm _____ amount taken

Time _____ am/pm _____ amount taken

Time _____ am/pm _____ amount taken

NAPS:

Time _____ am/pm Length of nap ……. Minutes

Time _____ am/pm Length of nap ……. Minutes

Time _____ am/pm Length of nap ……. Minutes

Time _____ am/pm Length of nap ……. Minutes

NOTES _____

_____

NOTES

MY BABY'S ROUTINE

FEEDING:

Time _____ am/pm _____ amount taken

Time _____ am/pm _____ amount taken

Time _____ am/pm _____ amount taken

Time _____ am/pm _____ amount taken

Time _____ am/pm _____ amount taken

Time _____ am/pm _____ amount taken

NAPS:

Time _____ am/pm Length of nap .... Minutes

Time _____ am/pm Length of nap .... Minutes

Time _____ am/pm Length of nap .... Minutes

Time _____ am/pm Length of nap .... Minutes

NOTES _____

_____

NOTES

_____

_____

_____

_____

_____

_____

_____

_____

_____

_____

_____

_____

_____

MY BABY'S ROUTINE

FEEDING:

Time _____ am/pm _____ amount taken

Time _____ am/pm _____ amount taken

Time _____ am/pm _____ amount taken

Time _____ am/pm _____ amount taken

Time _____ am/pm _____ amount taken

Time _____ am/pm _____ amount taken

NAPS:

Time _____ am/pm Length of nap .... Minutes

Time _____ am/pm Length of nap .... Minutes

Time _____ am/pm Length of nap .... Minutes

Time _____ am/pm Length of nap .... Minutes

NOTES _____

_____

NOTES

MY BABY'S ROUTINE

FEEDING:

Time _____ am/pm _____ amount taken

Time _____ am/pm _____ amount taken

Time _____ am/pm _____ amount taken

Time _____ am/pm _____ amount taken

Time _____ am/pm _____ amount taken

Time _____ am/pm _____ amount taken

NAPS:

Time _____ am/pm Length of nap .... Minutes

Time _____ am/pm Length of nap .... Minutes

Time _____ am/pm Length of nap .... Minutes

Time _____ am/pm Length of nap .... Minutes

NOTES _____

_____

NOTES _____

_____

_____

_____

_____

_____

_____

_____

_____

_____

_____

_____

_____

MY BABY'S ROUTINE

FEEDING:

Time _____ am/pm _____ amount taken

Time _____ am/pm _____ amount taken

Time _____ am/pm _____ amount taken

Time _____ am/pm _____ amount taken

Time _____ am/pm _____ amount taken

Time _____ am/pm _____ amount taken

NAPS:

Time _____ am/pm Length of nap .... Minutes

Time _____ am/pm Length of nap .... Minutes

Time _____ am/pm Length of nap .... Minutes

Time _____ am/pm Length of nap .... Minutes

NOTES _____

_____

NOTES

MY BABY'S ROUTINE

FEEDING:

Time _____ am/pm _____ amount taken

Time _____ am/pm _____ amount taken

Time _____ am/pm _____ amount taken

Time _____ am/pm _____ amount taken

Time _____ am/pm _____ amount taken

Time _____ am/pm _____ amount taken

NAPS:

Time _____ am/pm Length of nap .... Minutes

Time _____ am/pm Length of nap .... Minutes

Time _____ am/pm Length of nap .... Minutes

Time _____ am/pm Length of nap .... Minutes

NOTES _____

_____

MY BABY'S ROUTINE

FEEDING:

Time _____ am/pm _____ amount taken

Time _____ am/pm _____ amount taken

Time _____ am/pm _____ amount taken

Time _____ am/pm _____ amount taken

Time _____ am/pm _____ amount taken

Time _____ am/pm _____ amount taken

NAPS:

Time _____ am/pm Length of nap .... Minutes

Time _____ am/pm Length of nap .... Minutes

Time _____ am/pm Length of nap .... Minutes

Time _____ am/pm Length of nap .... Minutes

NOTES _____

_____

NOTES

MY BABY'S ROUTINE

FEEDING:

Time _____ am/pm _____ amount taken

Time _____ am/pm _____ amount taken

Time _____ am/pm _____ amount taken

Time _____ am/pm _____ amount taken

Time _____ am/pm _____ amount taken

Time _____ am/pm _____ amount taken

NAPS:

Time _____ am/pm Length of nap .... Minutes

Time _____ am/pm Length of nap .... Minutes

Time _____ am/pm Length of nap .... Minutes

Time _____ am/pm Length of nap .... Minutes

NOTES _____

_____

NOTES

MY BABY'S ROUTINE

FEEDING:

Time _____ am/pm _____ amount taken

Time _____ am/pm _____ amount taken

Time _____ am/pm _____ amount taken

Time _____ am/pm _____ amount taken

Time _____ am/pm _____ amount taken

Time _____ am/pm _____ amount taken

NAPS:

Time _____ am/pm Length of nap .... Minutes

Time _____ am/pm Length of nap .... Minutes

Time _____ am/pm Length of nap .... Minutes

Time _____ am/pm Length of nap .... Minutes

NOTES _____

_____

NOTES

MY BABY'S ROUTINE

FEEDING:

Time _____ am/pm _____ amount taken

Time _____ am/pm _____ amount taken

Time _____ am/pm _____ amount taken

Time _____ am/pm _____ amount taken

Time _____ am/pm _____ amount taken

Time _____ am/pm _____ amount taken

NAPS:

Time _____ am/pm Length of nap .... Minutes

Time _____ am/pm Length of nap .... Minutes

Time _____ am/pm Length of nap .... Minutes

Time _____ am/pm Length of nap .... Minutes

NOTES _____

_____

NOTES

MY BABY'S ROUTINE

FEEDING:

Time _____ am/pm _____ amount taken

Time _____ am/pm _____ amount taken

Time _____ am/pm _____ amount taken

Time _____ am/pm _____ amount taken

Time _____ am/pm _____ amount taken

Time _____ am/pm _____ amount taken

NAPS:

Time _____ am/pm Length of nap .... Minutes

Time _____ am/pm Length of nap .... Minutes

Time _____ am/pm Length of nap .... Minutes

Time _____ am/pm Length of nap .... Minutes

NOTES _____

_____

Printed in Great Britain
by Amazon